CONTENTS

CLAM CHOWDER

French fishermen invented this thick soup-stew, but New Englanders adopted it as their own, using the delicious varieties of clams found along their coastlines.

2lbs clams (1lb shelled or canned clams)
3oz rindless bacon, diced
2 medium onions, finely diced
1 tbsp flour
6 medium potatoes, peeled and cubed
Salt and pepper
4 cups milk
1 cup light cream
Chopped parsley (optional)

Step 2 Cook the bacon slowly until browned.

Step 1 Cook the clams until the shells open. Stir occasionally for even cooking.

Step 3 Cook the onion in the bacon fat until soft and transluscent.

1. Scrup the clams well and place them in a basin of cold water with a handful of flour to soak for 30 minutes. Drain the clams and place them in a deep saucepan with about ½ cup cold water. Cover and bring to the boil, stirring occasionally until all the shells open. Discard any shells that do not open. Strain the clam liquid and reserve it and set the clams aside to cool.

2. In a large, deep saucepan, over medium heat, cook bacon until browned. Remove it to paper towel to drain.

3. Add the onion to the bacon tat in the pan and cook slowly to soften. Stir in the flour and add the potatoes, salt, pepper, milk and reserved clam juice.

4. Cover and bring to the boil and then cook over a low heat for about 10 minutes, or until the potatoes are nearly tender. Remove the clams from their shells and chop them if large. Add to the soup along with the cream and diced bacon. Cook a further 10 minutes, or until the potatoes and clams are tender. Add the chopped parsley, if desired, and serve immediately.

Cook's Notes

Time
Preparation takes about 30 minutes and cooking takes about 30 minutes.

Cook's Tip
Soaking clams and other shellfish in water with flour or cornmeal before cooking plumps them up and also helps to eliminate sand and grit.

Serving Idea
Crumbled cooked bacon makes a delicious garnish for this chowder.

CORN AND POTATO CHOWDER

Such a filling soup, this is really a complete meal in a bowl.
Corn is a favorite ingredient in Southern cooking.

6 medium potatoes, peeled
Chicken or vegetable stock
1 onion, finely chopped
2 tbsps butter or margarine
4oz cooked ham, chopped
1 tbsp flour
4 ears fresh corn or about 4oz canned or frozen corn
3 cups milk
Salt and dash Tabasco
Finely chopped parsley

1. Quarter the potatoes and place them in a deep saucepan. Add stock to cover and the onion, and bring the mixture to the boil. Lower the heat and simmer, partially covered, until the potatoes are soft, about 15-20 minutes.

2. Drain the potatoes, reserving ¾ pint of the cooking liquid. Mash the potatoes and combine with reserved liquid.

3. Melt the butter or margarine in a clean pan, add the ham and cook briefly. Stir in the flour and pour over the potato mixture, mixing well.

4. If using fresh corn, remove the husks and silk and, holding one end of the corn, stand the ear upright. Use a large, sharp knife and cut against the cob vertically from top to bottom just scraping off the kernels. Add the corn and milk to the potato mixture and bring almost to the boil. Do not boil the corn rapidly as this will toughen it. Add a pinch of salt and a dash of Tabasco, and garnish with parsley before serving.

Step 3 Pour the potato mixture onto the flour and ham gradually, stirring constantly until well blended.

Step 4 Remove the husks and silk from the ears of corn.

Step 4 Use a sharp knife to cut the kernels off the cobs.

Cook's Notes

Time
Preparation takes about 25 minutes and cooking takes about 25-30 minutes.

Cook's Tip
When cooking corn on its own or adding it to other ingredients, add the salt just before serving. Cooking corn with salt toughens it.

Serving Idea
Serve with good country bread for a light lunch dish.

VIRGINIA PEANUT SOUP

Peanuts, popular all over the South, make a velvety rich soup
that is easily made from ordinary store cupboard ingredients.

4 tbsps butter or margarine
2 tbsps flour
1 cup creamy peanut butter
¼ tsp celery seed
2½ cups chicken stock
½ cup dry sherry
½ cup coarsely chopped peanuts

Step 4 Add the sherry to the soup before serving.

Step 2 Once the peanut butter and celery seed are added, gradually pour in the stock, stirring or whisking constantly.

1. Melt the butter or margarine in a saucepan over a medium heat. Remove from the heat and stir in the flour.

2. Add the peanut butter and celery seed. Gradually pour on the stock, stirring constantly.

3. Return the pan to a low heat and simmer gently for about 15 minutes, stirring occasionally. Do not allow to boil rapidly.

4. Stir in the sherry and ladle into a tureen or individual bowls. Sprinkle with the chopped peanuts.

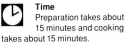

Cook's Notes

Time
Preparation takes about 15 minutes and cooking takes about 15 minutes.

Cook's Tip
The soup is slightly difficult to reheat, so it is best prepared just before serving.

Serving Idea
Croûtons (see garnish section) would also make a good garnish for this soup.

RED BEAN AND RED PEPPER SOUP

Red beans are very popular in southern Louisiana, and here they make a hearty soup combined with red peppers and red wine.

1lb dried red kidney beans
Water to cover
2 onions, coarsely chopped
3 sticks celery, coarsely chopped
2 bay leaves
Salt and pepper
3 large sweet red peppers, seeded and finely chopped
4 tbsps red wine
10 cups chicken stock
Lemon wedges and 4 chopped hard-cooked eggs to garnish

3. Bring to the boil over high heat and boil for 10 minutes, stirring occasionally. Reduce the heat to low and allow to simmer, partially covered, for about 3 hours, or until the beans are completely tender.

4. Remove the bay leaves and purée the soup in a food processor or blender.

5. Serve garnished with the chopped hard-cooked egg. Serve lemon wedges on the side.

Step 1 Soak the beans overnight in enough water to cover, or boil for two minutes and leave to soak for an hour. The beans will swell in size.

Step 2 Combine the beans with the other ingredients in a large stock pot and pour on enough chicken stock to cover.

Step 3 When the beans are soft enough to mash easily, remove bay leaves and purée the soup.

1. Soak the beans in the water overnight. Alternatively, bring them to the boil and boil rapidly for 2 minutes. Leave to stand for 1 hour.

2. Drain off the liquid and add the onions, celery, bay leaves, salt and pepper, sweet red peppers, red wine and stock.

Cook's Notes

Time
Preparation takes about 25 minutes, with overnight soaking for the beans. Cooking takes about 3 hours.

Cook's Tip
It is dangerous to eat dried pulses that are not thoroughly cooked. Make sure the beans are very soft before puréeing.

Serving Idea
Sour cream could be used in place of the hard-cooked eggs to garnish the soup.

CIOPPINO

California's famous and delicious fish stew is Italian in
heritage; but a close relative of French Bouillabaisse, too.

1lb spinach, well washed
1 tbsp each chopped fresh basil, thyme, rosemary and
  sage
2 tbsps chopped fresh marjoram
4 tbsps chopped parsley
1 large sweet red pepper, seeded and finely chopped
2 cloves garlic, crushed
24 large fresh clams or 48 mussels, well scrubbed
1 large crab, cracked
1lb monkfish
12 large shrimp, cooked and unpeeled
1lb canned plum tomatoes and juice
2 tbsps tomato paste
4 tbsps olive oil
Pinch salt and pepper
½-1 cup dry white wine
Water

Step 3 Place well
scrubbed clams or
mussels in the
bottom of a large
pot, sprinkling over
spinach mixture.

Step 6 Pour the
tomato paste and
wine mixture over
the layered seafood
and spinach.

1. Chop the spinach leaves roughly after removing any
tough stems.

2. Combine the spinach with the herbs, chopped sweet
red pepper and garlic, and set aside.

3. Discard any clams or mussels with broken shells or
ones that do not close when tapped. Place the shellfish in
the bottom of a large pot and sprinkle over a layer of the
spinach mixture.

4. Prepare the crab. Break off the claws and crack slightly.
Separate the body of the crab from the shell and pick out
the white meat. Discard the stomach sac and lungs.
Scrape out the brown meat, and place on top of the

spinach with the claws and white meat. Add another spinach layer.

5. Add the fish and a spinach layer, followed by the shrimp
and any remaining spinach.

6. Mix the tomatoes, tomato paste, oil, wine and seasonings and pour over the seafood and spinach.

7. Cover the pot, bring to the boil then reduce the heat to
low and simmer the mixture for about 40 minutes. If more
liquid is necessary, add water. Spoon into soup bowls, div-
iding the fish and shellfish evenly.

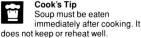

Cook's Notes

Time
Preparation takes about
40 minutes and cooking
takes about 40 minutes.

Cook's Tip
Soup must be eaten
immediately after cooking. It
does not keep or reheat well.

Serving Idea
This substantial fish stew
would serve six as a light
main course, served with good
bread.

SHRIMP BISQUE

This classic Cajun recipe makes a first course or a full meal. It isn't a smooth purée like its French counterpart.

3 tbsps butter or margarine
1 onion, finely chopped
1 sweet red pepper, seeded and finely chopped
2 sticks celery, finely chopped
1 clove garlic, minced
Pinch dry mustard and cayenne pepper
2 tsps paprika
3 tbsps flour
4 cups fish stock
1 sprig thyme and bay leaf
8oz raw, peeled shrimp
Salt and pepper
Snipped chives

3. Pour on the stock gradually, stirring until well blended. Add the thyme and bay leaf and bring to the boil. Reduce the heat to low and simmer for about 5 minutes or until thickened, stirring occasionally.

4. Add the shrimp and cook until pink and curled, about 5 minutes. Season with salt and pepper to taste and top with snipped chives before serving.

Step 3 Pour on the stock gradually and stir or beat with a whisk until well blended.

Step 2 Cook the mustard, cayenne, paprika and flour briefly until the mixture darkens in color.

Step 4 Use kitchen scissors to snip the chives finely over the top of the soup before serving.

1. Melt the butter or margarine over a low heat and add the onion, pepper, celery and garlic. Cook gently to soften.

2. Stir in the mustard, cayenne, paprika and flour. Cook about 3 minutes over a low heat, stirring occasionally.

Cook's Notes

Time Preparation takes about 20 minutes and cooking takes about 8-10 minutes.	

Time
Preparation takes about
20 minutes and cooking
takes about 8-10 minutes.

Cook's Tip
Cook spices such as
paprika briefly before
adding any liquid to develop their
flavor and eliminate harsh taste.

Serving Idea
Serve with garlic croûtons
(see garnish section) for
extra taste.

ZUCCHINI SOUP

The fresh taste of lemon and zucchini makes a delicious soup
that can be served either hot or cold.

1 medium-sized onion, thinly sliced
2½ tbsps olive oil
1lb zucchini, topped, tailed and sliced
Finely grated rind and juice of 1 large lemon
1¾ cups chicken stock
Freshly ground black pepper
2 egg yolks
¾ cup plain yogurt

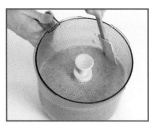

Step 4 Blend the soup in a blender or food processor until smooth.

Step 1 In a large pan, gently cook the onion until it is just transparent.

Step 5 Mix together the egg yolks and yogurt in a small jug or bowl.

1. In a large pan, cook the onion over a low heat in the olive oil for 3 minutes until it is just transparent.

2. Add the zucchini and cook for a further 2-3 minutes.

3. Stir in all remaining ingredients except the egg yolks and yogurt, cover and simmer for 20 minutes.

4. Transfer the soup to a blender or food processor, and blend until smooth.

5. Mix the egg yolks into the yogurt and stir into the blended soup.

6. Reheat the soup gently, stirring all the time until it thickens.

7. Serve hot at this stage, or transfer to a refrigerator and chill thoroughly.

Cook's Notes

Time
Preparation takes 20 minutes, plus chilling time, cooking takes 25 minutes.

Cook's Tip
Great care must be taken not to boil the soup once the egg yolks have been added, otherwise the mixture will curdle.

Serving Idea
Serve the soup with a garnish of thinly sliced zucchini and light French toasts.

CRAB AND CORN SOUP

This unusual soup is ideal either as an appetizer or,
with crusty whole-wheat bread, as a delicious lunch
or supper dish.

2 tbsps cornstarch
3 tbsps water
5 cups chicken stock
12oz corn
6oz crab meat, shredded
1 tsp soy sauce
Salt and pepper

Step 1 Blend the water and the cornstarch together in a small jug, or bowl, until it forms a smooth paste.

1. Blend the cornstarch and water together to form a smooth paste.

2. Put the stock into a large saucepan and bring this to the boil over a medium heat.

3. Add the sweetcorn, crab, soy sauce and seasoning to the stock. Bring to the boil again, reduce the heat to low

Step 3 Add the corn, crab, soy sauce and seasoning to the simmering stock.

Step 4 Remove the pan of simmering stock from the heat and gradually stir in the blended cornstarch. Return the pan to a gentle heat and bring back to the boil, stirring continuously, until the soup thickens.

and simmer for 4-5 minutes.

4. Remove the simmering stock from the heat and gradually add the blended cornstarch, stirring all the time. Return the pan to the heat and bring the soup back to the boil, stirring, until it thickens. Serve this soup hot.

 *Cook's Notes*

Time
Preparation takes about 8 minutes, and cooking also takes about 8 minutes.

Cook's Tip
This soup will freeze well, but must be thawed completely, then reheated thoroughly.

 Serving Idea
Beaten egg white can be stirred into the hot soup, just before serving, to create an authentic Chinese effect.

HOT AND SOUR SEAFOOD SOUP

This interesting combination of flavors and ingredients makes a sophisticated beginning to a meal.

3 dried Chinese mushrooms
Hot water
1 tbsp vegetable oil
¾ cup shrimp, cooked and peeled
1 hot red chili pepper, seeded and finely sliced
1 hot green chili pepper, seeded and finely sliced
½ tsp lemon rind, cut into thin slivers
2 green onions, sliced
2 cups fish stock
1 tbsp Worcestershire sauce
1 tbsp light soy sauce
2oz fish fillets
1 cake fresh bean curd, diced
1 tbsp lemon juice
1 tsp sesame seeds
Salt and pepper
1 tsp fresh coriander, finely chopped (optional)

Step 4 Remove the hard stalks from the reconstituted Chinese mushrooms and discard them. Slice the caps finely.

Step 5 Add the diced fish together with the bean curd and shredded mushroom caps to the soup mixture.

1. Soak the mushrooms in enough hot water to cover for 20 minutes, or until completely reconstituted.

2. Heat the vegetable oil in a large wok or skillet over a high heat and add the shrimp, chili peppers, lemon rind and green onions. Stir-fry quickly for 1 minute.

3. Add the stock, the Worcestershire sauce and the soy sauce. Bring this mixture to the boil, reduce the heat to low and simmer for 5 minutes. Season to taste.

4. Remove the hard stalks from the mushrooms and discard them. Slice the caps very finely.

5. Cut the fish fillets into small dice, and add them to the soup, together with the bean curd and Chinese mushrooms. Simmer for a further 5 minutes.

6. Stir in the lemon juice and sesame seeds. Adjust the seasoning and serve sprinkled with chopped fresh coriander leaves, if desired.

Cook's Notes

Time
Preparation takes about 20 minutes, and cooking also takes about 20 minutes.

Cook's Tip
Dried Chinese mushrooms and fresh bean curd cakes can be bought in most delicatessens, or ethnic supermarkets.

Serving Idea
This soup has a hot flavor and is best served with something mild, such as Chinese shrimp crackers.

SPICED SOUP

Spicy and fragrant, this warming Indonesian soup is a
meal in itself.

4-8 tbsps oil
1 clove garlic, peeled but left whole
1lb chicken breast, skinned, boned and cut into small
    pieces
1 cake fresh bean curd, diced
½ cup raw cashew nuts
4 shallots, roughly chopped
1 carrot, very thinly sliced
3oz snow peas
2oz Chinese noodles, soaked for 5 minutes in hot water
    and drained thoroughly
5 cups vegetable or chicken stock
Juice of 1 lime
¼ tsp turmeric
2 curry leaves
1 tsp grated fresh ginger
1 tbsp soy sauce
Salt and pepper

Step 2 Stir the chicken pieces into the hot oil, and stir-fry them until they begin to brown.

Step 6 Cook the noodles on one side, until they have browned. Turn them over to brown the other side.

1. Heat some of the oil in a wok or large skillet over a medium heat. Add the garlic and cook until brown. Remove the garlic from the pan and discard.

2. Add the chicken pieces and cook in the oil, until they begin to brown. Remove the pieces and drain well.

3. Add a little more oil and cook the bean curd until lightly browned. Remove and drain well.

4. Add the cashews and cook, stirring constantly until toasted. Remove and drain well.

5. Add a little more oil and cook the shallots and carrot until lightly browned. Stir in the snow peas and cook for 1 minute. Remove from the pan and drain.

6. Turn up the heat, and heat the remaining oil in the wok until it is very hot, adding any remaining from the original amount. Add the noodles and cook quickly until brown on one side. Turn over and brown the other side.

7. Lower the heat and pour in the stock. Stir in the lime juice, turmeric, curry leaves, ginger, soy sauce and seasoning. Cover and simmer gently over a low heat for about 10 minutes, stirring occasionally, to prevent the noodles from sticking.

8. Return all the cooked ingredients to the pan and heat through for 5 minutes. Serve immediately.

Cook's Notes

Time
Preparation takes about 20 minutes and cooking takes about 20-25 minutes.

Cook's Tip
If it is not possible to buy raw cashew nuts, use well rinsed and dried salted cashew nuts, and do not fry them in the oil.

Serving Idea
Substitute 8oz of button or, if obtainable, wild mushrooms and 4oz shredded Chinese leaves in place of the chicken and vegetable stock, to make a delicious vegetarian meal.

TOMATO SOUP

This healthy version of a firm family favorite is high in fiber, low
in fat and hearty enough to be a complete meal in itself.

4oz whole-wheat macaroni
1 tbsp sunflower oil
1 small onion, chopped
1 small green pepper, seeded and chopped
2 tbsps whole-wheat flour
4 cups vegetable stock
1lb fresh tomatoes, cored and finely chopped
2 tbsps tomato paste
1 tbsp grated horseradish
Salt and pepper

Step 3 Add the stock to the onion, pepper and flour mixture gradually, stirring well between additions to ensure that the soup is smooth.

Step 2 Stir the onion and pepper into the hot oil, mixing well to coat them evenly.

Step 5 Pour the tomato mixture into a blender or food processor and blend for about 30 seconds, or until the tomatoes have been completely broken down.

1. Cook the macaroni in enough boiling salted water to cover for about 15 minutes, or until it is just soft. Drain and rinse the macaroni in cold water, then set aside until required.

2. In a large saucepan heat the oil until it is hot. Stir in the onion and the pepper, cover the pan and cook for 3-4 minutes over a medium heat.

3. Stir the flour into the onion mixture and add the stock gradually, stirring well between additions.

4. Add the tomatoes, the tomato paste and the horseradish, and simmer over a low heat for 15 minutes.

5. Put the tomato mixture into a blender or food processor and process for about 30 seconds, or until smooth. Return the soup to the saucepan and season with salt and pepper to taste.

6. Add the macaroni to the soup and simmer over a low heat for 10 minutes before serving.

Cook's Notes

Time
Preparation takes about 15 minutes, and cooking takes about 45 minutes.

Cook's Tip
If you do not have a blender or food processor, you can push the tomato soup through a wire sieve, using a metal spoon. However, this does have the disadvantage of removing the tomato skins and pips, which are an excellent source of fiber.

Serving Idea
Serve the soup topped with 1 dessertspoon of fromage frais, or plain yogurt and a sprinkling of chopped fresh parsley or basil.

GAZPACHO

A typically Spanish soup, this is the perfect summer first
course. The recipe comes from Andalusia, in southern Spain.

1 medium green pepper, seeded and roughly chopped
8 medium tomatoes, peeled, seeded and roughly
    chopped
1 large cucumber, peeled and roughly chopped
1 large onion, roughly chopped
3-5oz French bread, crusts removed
3 tbsps red wine vinegar
3 cups water
Pinch salt and pepper
1-2 cloves garlic, crushed
3 tbsps olive oil
2 tsps tomato paste (optional)

Garnish
1 small onion, diced
½ small cucumber diced, but not peeled
3 tomatoes, peeled, seeded and diced
½ green pepper, seeded and diced

Step 2 Add the
liquid, seasoning
and garlic and stir
the mixture well.

Step 4 After
puréeing the soup,
pour back into a
bowl and beat in the
olive oil by hand.

1. Combine all the prepared vegetables in a deep bowl
and add the bread, breaking it into small pieces by hand.
Mix together thoroughly.

2. Add the vinegar, water, salt, pepper and garlic.

3. Pour the mixture, a third at a time, into a blender or food
processor and purée for about 1 minute, or until the soup is
smooth.

4. Pour the purée into a clean bowl and gradually beat in
the olive oil using a whisk. Add enough tomato paste for a
good red color.

5. Cover the bowl tightly and refrigerate for at least 2
hours, or until thoroughly chilled. Before serving, beat the
soup to make sure all the ingredients are blended and then
pour into a large chilled soup tureen or into chilled individual soup bowls. Serve all the garnishes in separate bowls
to be added to the soup if desired.

Cook's Notes

 Cook's Tip
Gazpacho may be prepared
a day in advance and kept
overnight in the refrigerator. To
quickly chill the soup, omit 1 cup
water from the recipe and use
crushed ice instead. Leave
refrigerated for 30 minutes, stirring
frequently to melt the ice.

 Time
Preparation takes about
20 minutes and the soup
must chill for at least 2 hours.

Serving Idea
Garnish with croûtons (see
garnish section) in place of
the diced vegetables.

SERVES 6-8

WONTON SOUP

Probably the best-known Chinese soup, this recipe uses
store-bought wonton wrappers for ease of preparation.

20-24 wonton wrappers
3oz finely ground chicken or pork
2 tbsps chopped Chinese parsley
3 green onions, finely chopped
1-inch piece fresh ginger, peeled and grated
1 egg, lightly beaten
5 cups chicken stock
1 tbsp dark soy sauce
Dash sesame oil
Salt and pepper
Chinese parsley or watercress for garnish.

Step 2 Place a spoonful of filling on half of each wrapper.

Step 3 Fold over the tops and press firmly with the fingers to seal.

Step 1 Place the wonton wrappers out on a clean surface. Brush edges with beaten egg.

1. Place all the wonton wrappers on a large, flat surface. Mix together the chicken or pork, chopped parsley, green onions and ginger. Brush the edges of the wrappers lightly with beaten egg.

2. Place a small mound of mixture on one half of the wrap-

pers and fold the other half over the top to form a triangle.

3. Press with the fingers to seal the edges well.

4. Bring the stock to the boil in a large saucepan. Add the filled wontons, reduce the heat to low and simmer 5-10 minutes or until they float to the surface. Add remaining ingredients to the soup, using only the leaves of the parsley or watercress for garnish.

Cook's Notes

Time
Preparation takes 25-30 minutes and cooking takes about 5-10 minutes.

Cook's Tip
Wonton wrappers are sometimes called wonton skins. They are available in specialty shops, delicatessens and Chinese supermarkets. Chinese parsley is also known as coriander or cilantro and is available from greengrocers and supermarkets.

Serving Idea
Small green onion flowers also make an attractive garnish for this soup.

SERVES 4

BEEF AND BEAN SOUP

In Mexico, where the day's main meal is eaten at around
2.00 pm, this soup is a popular appetizer.

1 large onion, peeled and finely chopped
2 sticks celery, chopped
1 sweet red pepper, seeded and finely chopped
2 tbsps oil
8oz ground beef
6 tomatoes, peeled, seeded and chopped
15oz canned refried beans
1 tsp ground cumin
1 tsp chili powder
1 tsp garlic powder or paste
Pinch cinnamon and cayenne pepper
Salt and pepper
2 cups beef stock (see basic recipes)

Step 2 Cook the beef over medium heat until well browned.

Step 4 Purée the soup in several batches until nearly smooth.

Step 1 Cook the onion, celery and pepper in oil to soften. Stir frequently.

1. Cook the onion, pepper and celery in the oil in a large saucepan over a low heat until softened.

2. Add the beef and cook over medium heat until well browned. Add the tomatoes and refried beans with the spices, garlic and seasoning and mix well.

3. Stir in the stock and bring to the boil. Cover, reduce the heat to low and simmer gently for 30 minutes, stirring occasionally.

4. Pour the soup into a blender or food processor and purée. The soup will be quite thick and not completely smooth.

Cook's Notes

Time
Preparation takes about 20 minutes and cooking takes about 50 minutes in total.

Cook's Tip
Make sure the blender or food processor lid is closed securely before puréeing the hot soup. Purée in 2 or 3 small batches for safety.

Serving Idea
Top the soup with sour cream and serve with tortilla chips.

CREAM OF PUMPKIN SOUP

Pumpkins have an honored place in American culinary history and show up in many different preparations. Their excellent color and texture make a distinctive soup.

1 large pumpkin about 4-5lbs in weight
¼ cup butter or margarine
1 large onion, sliced
1 cup heavy cream
Pinch salt, white pepper and nutmeg
Snipped chives to garnish, optional

1. Wash the pumpkin well on the outside and cut through horizontally, about 2 inches down from the stem end.

2. Carefully cut most of the flesh off the top and reserve the lid for later use.

3. Remove the seeds and stringy pulp from the inside and discard them.

4. Using a small, sharp knife, carefully remove all but ½ inch of the flesh from inside the pumpkin. Work slowly and carefully to avoid piercing the outer skin of the pumpkin. Chop all the flesh from the top of the pumpkin and the inside and set it aside.

5. Melt the butter or margarine in a large saucepan over a low heat and add the onion. Cook slowly until the onion is tender but not brown. Add the pumpkin flesh and about 4 cups cold water. Bring to the boil and then reduce the heat to low and allow to simmer gently, covered, for about 20 minutes.

6. Purée the mixture in a food processor or blender in several small batches. Return the soup to the pot and add the cream, salt, pepper and nutmeg to taste. Reheat the soup over a low heat and pour it into the reserved pumpkin shell. Garnish the top of the soup with snipped chives, if desired, before serving.

Step 1 Using a large, sharp knife, cut the top off the pumpkin to serve as a lid.

Step 3 Remove the seeds and stringy pulp from inside the pumpkin and discard.

Step 4 Using a small, sharp knife, work slowly to remove the flesh from inside the pumpkin. Leave some flesh on the skin to form a shell.

 *Cook's Notes*

 Time
Preparation takes about 45 minutes, and cooking takes about 35-40 minutes.

 Cook's Tip
If desired, 2 pumpkins may be used, 1 for making the soup and 1 to serve as a tureen. The pumpkin used for cooking must be peeled first.

Serving Idea
The soup may be served in a tureen or individual bowls instead of the pumpkin shell, if preferred.

ONION SOUP

A wholesome, warming soup for cold winter days.

Step 1 Brown the onions in a large saucepan with butter and sugar.

¼ cup butter or margarine
2lbs onions, thinly sliced
2 tsps sugar
1½ tbsps flour
7 cups brown stock (see basic recipes)
½ cup dry white wine
Salt and pepper
1 tsp dried thyme

Croûtes
12 1-inch slices French bread
1 tbsp olive oil
2 cups grated Gruyère cheese

Step 3 Brush both sides of bread with olive oil and bake until lightly brown.

1. Melt the butter in a large saucepan over a moderate heat. Stir in the onions and add the sugar. Cook, uncovered, over low heat, stirring occasionally, for 20-30 minutes or until the onions are golden brown.

2. Sprinkle the flour over the onions and cook for 2-3 minutes. Pour on the stock and the wine and stir to blend with the flour. Add salt, pepper and thyme and return the soup to low heat. Simmer, partially covered, for another 30-40 minutes. Allow the soup to stand while preparing the croûtes.

Step 4 Place the croûtes on soup and sprinkle with cheese before baking in a hot oven until the cheese melts.

3. Brush each side of the slices of bread lightly with olive oil and place them on a baking sheet. Bake in a preheated oven, 325°F, for about 15 minutes. Turn the slices over and bake for a further 15 minutes, or until the bread is dry and lightly browned.

4. To serve, skim any fat from the soup and ladle soup into an ovenproof tureen or individual soup bowls. Place the croûtes on top of the soup and sprinkle over the grated cheese. Place the soup in a hot oven, 400°F, and bake for 10-20 minutes, or until the cheese has melted. Brown under a preheated broiler, if desired, before serving.

Cook's Notes

Time
Preparation takes about 20 minutes. Cooking takes about 2 hours in total.

Cook's Tip
The addition of sugar helps the onions to brown.

Serving Idea
This soup is very filling and is best followed by a light main course.

CAPE COD MUSSELS

When seafood is as good as that from Cape Cod, even the simplest preparations stand out.

4½lbs mussels in their shells
Flour or cornmeal
1 cup dry white wine
1 large onion, finely chopped
2-4 cloves garlic, finely chopped
Salt and pepper
2 bay leaves
1 cup butter, melted
Juice of 1 lemon

1. Scrub the mussels well and remove any barnacles and beards (seaweed strands). Use a stiff brush to scrub the shells, and discard any mussels with broken shells or those that do not close when tapped.

2. Place the mussels in a basin full of cold water with a handful of flour or cornmeal and leave to soak for 30 minutes.

3. Drain the mussels and place them in a large, deep saucepan with the remaining ingredients, except the butter and lemon juice. Cover the pan and bring to the boil over a medium heat.

4. Stir the mussels occasionally while they are cooking to help them cook evenly. Cook about 5-8 minutes, or until the shells open. Discard any mussels that do not open.

5. Spoon the mussels into individual serving bowls and strain the cooking liquid. Pour the liquid into 4 small bowls and serve with the mussels and a bowl of melted butter mixed with lemon juice for each person. Dip the mussels into the broth and the melted butter to eat. Use a mussel shell to pinch out each mussel, or eat with small forks or spoons.

Step 1 Scrub the mussels with a stiff brush to remove barnacles and seaweed beards.

Step 1 To test if the mussels are still alive, tap them on a work surface – the shells should close.

Step 5 Hold an empty mussel shell between 2 fingers and pinch together to remove mussels from their shells to eat.

Cook's Notes

Time
Preparation takes about 40 minutes, and cooking takes about 5-8 minutes.

Cook's Tip
The beards are strands of seaweed that anchor the mussels to the rocks on which they grow. These must be removed before cooking. They can be pulled off quite easily by hand, or scrubbed off with a stiff brush.

Serving Idea
Chopped fresh herbs may be added to the broth.

CRAB MEATBALLS

These delicious, mildly spicy crab meatballs can be made
ahead, then coated and fried at the last minute.

1lb fresh or frozen crab meat, chopped finely
4 slices white bread, crusts removed and made into
    crumbs
1 tbsp butter or margarine
1 tbsp flour
½ cup milk
½ mild green chili pepper, seeded and finely chopped
1 green onion, finely chopped
1 tbsp chopped parsley
Salt
Flour
2 eggs, beaten
Dry bread crumbs
Oil

Step 4 Flour hands
well and shape cold
crab mixture into
balls.

Step 5 Brush on
beaten egg or dip
into egg to coat.

1. Combine the crab meat with the fresh breadcrumbs and
set aside.

2. Melt the butter and add the flour off the heat. Stir in the
milk and return to moderate heat. Bring to the boil, stirring
constantly.

3. Stir the white sauce into the crab meat and breadcrumbs, adding the chili, onion and parsley. Season with
salt to taste, cover and allow to cool completely.

4. Shape the cold mixture into 1-inch balls with floured
hands.

5. Coat with beaten egg using a fork to turn balls in the
mixture or use a pastry brush to coat with egg.

6. Coat with the dry bread crumbs.

7. Cook in oil in a deep sauté pan, wok or deep-fat fryer at
365°F until golden brown and crisp, about 3 minutes per
batch of 6. Turn occasionally while cooking.

8. Drain on paper towels and sprinkle lightly with salt.

Cook's Notes

Time
Preparation takes about
40-50 minutes, including
time for the mixture to cool. A batch
of 6 balls takes about 3 minutes to
cook.

Cook's Tip
Cooked haddock can be
substituted for half of the
crab meat. Crab sticks can also be
used.

Serving Idea
Serve the crabmeat balls as
a cocktail snack.

OYSTERS ROCKEFELLER

Oysters can be purchased already opened, and you'll find
the rest of this famous New Orleans dish simplicity itself to
prepare.

24 oysters on the half shell
Rock salt
6 strips bacon, finely chopped
1¼lbs fresh spinach, well washed, stems removed and
  leaves finely chopped
1 small bunch green onions, finely chopped
2 cloves garlic, crushed
4-5 tbsps fine fresh bread crumbs
Dash Tabasco
2 tbsps aniseed liqueur
Pinch salt
Parmesan cheese

1. Loosen the oysters from their shells, strain and reserve
their liquid.

2. Rinse the shells well and return an oyster to each one.
Pour about 1 inch of rock salt into a baking pan and place in
the oysters in their shells, pressing each shell gently into
the salt.

3. In a skillet over medium heat, cook the bacon until
browned.

4. Add the spinach, green onions and garlic and cook
slowly over a low heat until softened. Add the bread
crumbs, Tabasco, oyster liquid, liqueur, and a pinch of salt.

5. Spoon some of the mixture onto each oyster and sprinkle with Parmesan cheese. Place in a preheated 350°F
oven for about 15 minutes. Alternatively, heat through in the
oven for 10 minutes and place under a preheated broiler to
lightly brown the cheese. Serve immediately.

Step 1 With a small
sharp knife, loosen
the oysters from
their shells to make
them easier to eat.
Hold over bowl to
catch liquid.

Step 2 Press the
oyster shells into a
baking pan filled
with salt so that the
shells sit level.

Step 5 Spoon in the
prepared mixture to
cover each oyster
completely.

Cook's Notes

 Time
Preparation takes about
25 minutes or longer if
opening the oysters yourself.
Cooking takes about 25 minutes.

Cook's Tip
Fishmongers will sell
oysters already opened on
their half shell. If only shelled oysters
are available, allow 6 per person and
cook them 6 at a time in small baking
dishes.

 Serving Idea
Use finely-chopped
anchovies instead of the
bacon, and substitute 3 tbsps butter
or margarine for the bacon fat.

CRAB MEAT IMPERIAL

Another famous New Orleans dish, this makes a delicious warm weather salad for lunches, light suppers or elegant appetizers.

2 small crabs, boiled
2 tbsps oil
4 green onions
1 small green pepper, seeded and finely chopped
1 stick celery, finely chopped
1 clove garlic, crushed
¾ cup prepared mayonnaise (see basic recipes)
1 tbsp mild mustard
Dash Tabasco and Worcestershire sauce
1 piece canned pimento, drained and finely chopped
Salt and pepper
2 tbsps chopped parsley
Lettuce, curly endive or radicchio (optional)

1. To shell the crabs, first remove all the legs and the large claws by twisting and pulling them away from the body.

2. Turn the shell over and, using your thumbs, push the body away from the flat shell. Set the body aside.

3. Remove the stomach sack and the lungs or dead man's fingers and discard them. Using a small teaspoon, scrape the brown body meat out of the flat shell.

4. Using a sharp knife, cut the body of the crab in four pieces and using a pick or a skewer, push out all the meat.

5. Crack the large claws and remove the meat in one piece if possible. Crack the legs and remove the meat as well, leaving the small, thin legs in the shell. Set all the meat aside. Scrub the shells to use for serving if desired.

6. Heat the oil in a small sauté pan or skillet. Chop the white parts of the green onions and add to the oil with the green pepper, celery and garlic. Sauté over a low heat for about 10 minutes, stirring often to soften the vegetables but not brown them. Remove from the heat and set aside. When cool, add the mayonnaise, mustard, Tabasco, Wor-

cestershire sauce, pimento and finely chopped tops of the green onions.

7. Spoon the reserved brown body meat from the crabs back into each shell or serving dish. Mix the remaining crab meat with the dressing, reserving the crab claws for garnish, if desired. They may also be shredded and added to the other crab meat. Do not overmix the sauce as the crab meat should stay in large pieces. Spoon into the shells on top of the brown body meat, sprinkle with chopped parsley and place the crab shells on serving plates, surrounding them with lettuce leaves, if desired. Garnish with the shelled crab claws and use the crab legs if desired. Serve immediately.

Step 3 Discard the plastic-like stomach sack and spongy lungs. Remove brown body meat from the shell of the crab and reserve it.

Step 4 Cut through the body of the crab with a sharp knife and pick out the crab meat with a skewer.

Cook's Notes

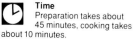

Time
Preparation takes about 45 minutes, cooking takes about 10 minutes.

Cook's Tip
If desired, recipe can be prepared with dressed or frozen crab meat. Allow about 3-4 oz crab meat per person.

Serving Idea
This dish makes a lovely lunch or light supper for two, served with French bread and a green salad.

SMOKED SALMON STUFFED CUCUMBERS

This exquisite appetizer will soon become a firm favorite.

1 large cucumber
Salt for sprinkling
4oz smoked salmon
1 cup ricotta or cream cheese
2 tsps finely chopped fresh chives
½ cup plain yogurt
2 tbsps whipping cream
2 tsps finely chopped fresh dill
Squeeze of lemon juice
Salt and pepper
1 head of iceberg lettuce
Red caviar, to garnish

Step 1 Cut the cucumber in half lengthwise and carefully scoop out the seeds using a serrated grapefruit spoon or knife.

Step 4 Pipe the salmon mixture evenly into the hollow left in the cucumber by the removal of the seeds.

Step 5 Use a sharp knife to cut the chilled stuffed cucumber carefully into ¼-inch slices.

1. Cut the cucumber in half lengthwise and scoop out the seeds. Sprinkle the surface with salt and leave to stand for 1 hour.

2. Work the smoked salmon and the cheese in a blender until smooth. Stir in the chives.

3. Mix the yogurt, cream and dill together, adding lemon juice and seasoning to taste.

4. Rinse the cucumber thoroughly and pat as dry as possible. Using a pastry bag, fitted with a ½-inch plain nozzle, pipe the smoked salmon mixture into the hollow left in the cucumber, sandwich the two halves together firmly, wrap tightly in polythene or plastic wrap and chill for at least 1 hour.

5. Arrange the lettuce leaves on serving plates. Unwrap the cucumber, trim away the ends and slice carefully into ¼-inch slices. Arrange these on top of the lettuce.

6. Spoon a little of the yogurt mixture over each and garnish with a little red caviar.

Cook's Notes

Time
Preparation takes about 15 minutes, but allow at least 1 hour for chilling, before serving. The cucumber must also stand for 1 hour.

Cook's Tip
Use halved, hard-cooked eggs, with the yolks removed, instead of the cucumber. The yolks can be sieved over the dressing instead of the caviar, if preferred.

Serving Idea
Use the slices of stuffed cucumber, without the yogurt dressing, as part of a tray of hors d'oeuvres.

SHRIMP PASTRY PUFFS

These light pastry puffs are excellent savory snacks for a
picnic or informal party.

6 tbsps butter
⅓ cup water
Generous ¾ cup all-purpose flour, sifted
3 eggs, beaten
3 tbsps butter
6 tbsps flour
1 cup milk
2 tbsps white wine
1 bay leaf
1 cup peeled shrimp, chopped
2 hard-cooked eggs, chopped
Pinch nutmeg
1 tsp chopped fresh dill
Salt and pepper

Step 2 Beat the eggs vigorously into the flour and water mixture, adding them gradually, until a smooth, shiny paste is formed.

Step 6 Cut the puffs almost in half through the middle and fill each cavity with the shrimp and egg mixture.

1. Put the 6 tbsps butter and the water into a saucepan. Bring to the boil over a medium heat. Tip in the ¾ cup flour all at once and beat, until the mixture is smooth and leaves the sides of the pan clean. Remove from the heat and leave to cool slightly.

2. Add the eggs gradually to the flour mixture, beating vigorously, until they are well incorporated and the mixture forms a smooth, shiny paste.

3. Line a cookie sheet with silicone paper and drop heaped teaspoonfuls of the mixture onto it, spaced well apart. Bake in a prehated oven, 400°F, for 25 minutes, or until the pastry puffs are firm to the touch and golden brown.

4. Melt the remaining butter in a saucepan over a medium

heat and stir in the remaining flour. Blend in the milk gradually, beating well between additions. When all the milk is mixed in, add the wine and bay leaf and bring to the boil, stirring constantly.

5. Remove the bay leaf and stir in the remaining ingredients.

6. Cut the pastry puffs almost in half through the middle and fill with the shrimp and egg mixture.

Cook's Notes

 Time
Preparation will take about 15 minutes and cooking takes about 30-35 minutes.

 Cook's Tip
To make sure that the pastry puffs stay crisp, after cooking is complete, make a small slit in the side of each puff and return them to the oven, with the heat switched off, for 5 minutes, so that they dry out completely.

Serving Idea
For a party, decorate the tray carrying the puffs with a citrus basket stuffed with shrimp (see garnish section).

FISH TEMPURA

This is a traditional Japanese dish, which can be served as an unusual appetizer.

12 uncooked large shrimp
¼lb halibut or flounder, skinned and cut into 2 × ¾-inch strips
Small whole fish, e.g. silversides, sand eels, or herring
2 squid, cleaned and cut into strips 1 × 3 inches long
2 tbsps all-purpose flour, for dusting
1 egg yolk
Scant ½ cup iced water
1 cup all-purpose flour
Oil
6 tbsps soy sauce
Juice and finely grated rind of 2 limes
4 tbsps dry sherry

1. Shell the shrimp, leaving the tails intact. Wash the fish and the squid and pat dry. Dust them all with the 2 tbsps flour.

2. Make a batter by beating together the egg yolk and water. Sift in the cup of all-purpose flour and mix well with a fork.

3. Dip each piece of fish into the batter, shaking off any excess.

4. In a wok or deep-fat fryer, heat the oil to 365°F or until it is hot enough to brown a 1-inch cube of bread in 60 seconds. Lower in the fish pieces a few at a time and cook for 2-3 minutes. Lift them out carefully and drain on paper towels, keeping warm until required.

5. Mix together the soy sauce, lime juice, rind and sherry and serve as a dip with the cooked fish.

Step 2 The batter will be lumpy and look undermixed.

Step 3 Do not batter too many pieces of fish at a time. Only coat those you are about to cook.

Step 4 Cook only 3 or 4 pieces and only one kind of fish at a time.

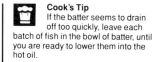
Cook's Notes

Time
Preparation takes about 30 minutes and cooking time varies from 2 to 3 minutes per batch, depending on the type of fish.

Cook's Tip
If the batter seems to drain off too quickly, leave each batch of fish in the bowl of batter, until you are ready to lower them into the hot oil.

Serving Idea
Garnish with radish water lilies (see garnish section) for a very delicate, Japanese look to the dish.

SEVICHE

Do not be put off by the thought of eating raw fish, as the cod
will "cook" in the marinade. The result is delicious – spicy
without being too hot.

1lb cod fillets
Juice and grated rind of 2 limes
1 shallot, chopped
1 green chili pepper, seeded and finely chopped
1 tsp ground coriander
1 small green pepper, seeded and sliced
1 small sweet red pepper, seeded and sliced
1 tbsp chopped fresh parsley
1 tbsp chopped fresh coriander leaves
4 green onions, chopped
2 tbsps olive oil
Salt and pepper
1 small lettuce

Step 2 Stir the lime juice and rind, together with the shallot and spices, into the strips of cod, mixing thoroughly to coat them evenly with the spice mixture.

Step 4 Stir the peppers, herbs, onion and oil into the drained fish.

Step 1 Cut the skinned cod fillets into thin strips across the grain, removing any bones you may find.

1. Skin the cod fillets and cut them into thin strips across the grain.

2. Put the cod strips into a bowl, pour over the lime juice

and rind. Add the shallot, chili pepper and coriander, and stir well to coat the fish completely.

3. Cover the bowl and refrigerate for 24 hours, stirring occasionally.

4. When ready to serve, drain the fish and stir in the peppers, parsley, coriander leaves, onions and oil. Season to taste and serve on a bed of lettuce.

Cook's Notes

Time
Preparation takes about 20 minutes, plus 24 hours' refrigeration.

Cook's Tip
Substitute haddock or monkfish fillets for the cod.

Serving Ideas
Serve with crusty French bread or tortilla chips.

SALMON PÂTÉ

This highly nutritious, elegant pâté is low in fat and very quick
to prepare.

8oz canned red or pink salmon, drained
½ cup low fat cream or ricotta cheese
Few drops lemon juice
Pinch ground mace, or ground nutmeg
¼ tsp Tabasco sauce
Salt and pepper
2 tbsps fromage frais, or plain yogurt
4 small pickles

---

1. Remove any bones and skin from the salmon. In a bowl, work the fish into a smooth paste with the back of a spoon.

2. Beat the cheese until it is smooth.

3. Add the salmon, lemon juice, seasonings, and fromage frais or plain yogurt to the cheese and mix well, until thoroughly incorporated.

4. Divide the mixture equally between 4 individual custard cups. Smooth the surfaces carefully.

5. Slice each pickle lengthways, 4 or 5 times, making sure that you do not cut completely through it at the narrow end. Splay the cut ends into a fan, and use these to decorate the tops of the pâtés in the custard cups.

Step 1 Put the salmon into a small bowl and work it with the back of a spoon, until it becomes a smooth paste.

Step 5 Slice each pickle lengthwise 4 or 5 times, taking great care not to cut right through the pickle at the narrow end. Spread each of the cut ends out carefully into a fan shape. Use these to garnish the tops of the pâtés.

Cook's Notes

Time
Preparation takes about 15 minutes.

Cook's Tip
If you have a food processor or blender, you can work the cheese and salmon together in this, instead of beating them in a bowl.

Serving Idea
Serve with toast, or crispy whole-wheat rolls.

SHRIMP ACAPULCO

These make a stylish appetizer or a quickly prepared snack.

4 slices bread, crusts removed
6 tbsps softened butter
6oz cooked and peeled shrimp
½ tsp chili powder
¼ tsp paprika
¼ tsp cumin
Salt and pepper
Watercress to garnish

Step 2 Cook the bread on a baking sheet until golden brown and crisp.

Step 3 Cook the shrimp and chili mixture over a low heat, stirring continuously.

1. Cut the bread slices in half and use 2 tbsps of the butter to butter both sides sparingly.

2. Place the bread on a baking sheet and cook in a pre-heated 350°F oven for 10-15 minutes until golden brown. Keep warm.

3. Melt the remaining butter in a small pan over a low heat and add the shrimp, spices and seasoning and stir well.

4. Heat through completely and spoon on top of the bread slices. Garnish with watercress and serve hot.

Cook's Notes

Time
Preparation takes about 15 minutes. The bread will take 15-20 minutes to cook until golden, and the shrimp take about 5 minutes to heat through.

Cook's Tip
The bread may be prepared in advance and reheated 5 minutes in the oven. Do not reheat the shrimp.

Serving Idea
Make the bread slices smaller to serve with cocktails.

JEKYLL ISLAND SHRIMP

Named after an island off the Georgia coast, this makes a rich
appetizer.

2lbs cooked shrimp
4 tbsps butter, softened
Pinch salt, white pepper and cayenne
1 clove garlic, crushed
6 tbsps fine dry breadcrumbs
2 tbsps chopped parsley
4 tbsps sherry
Lemon wedges or slices

Step 2 Pull off the tail shell and carefully remove the very end.

Step 1 Remove the heads and legs from the shrimp first. Remove any roe at this time.

Step 6 Spread the mixture to completely cover the shrimp.

1. To prepare the shrimp, remove the heads and legs first.

2. Peel off the shells, carefully removing the tail shells.

3. Remove the black vein running down the length of the rounded side with a wooden pick.

4. Arrange shrimp in a shallow casserole or individual dishes.

5. Combine the remaining ingredients, except the lemon garnish, mixing well.

6. Spread the mixture to completely cover the shrimp and place in a preheated 375°F oven for about 20 minutes, or until the butter melts and the crumbs become crisp. Garnish with lemon wedges or slices.

Cook's Notes

 Time
Prepration takes about 35-40 minutes and cooking takes about 20 minutes.

 **Cook's Tip**
Freshly cooked shrimp are available from most fishmongers. Frozen shrimp will not be as good.

 Serving Idea
Serve with garlic bread and a salad.

FRIED FISH WITH GARLIC SAUCE

Fish in such an attractive shape makes an excellent first course.

1 cup all-purpose flour
Pinch salt
4-6 tbsps cold water
Oil
2lbs fresh anchovies or whitebait

Garlic Sauce
4 slices bread, crusts trimmed, soaked in water for 10 minutes
4 cloves garlic, peeled and roughly chopped
2 tbsps lemon juice
4-5 tbsps olive oil
1-2 tbsps water (optional)
Salt and pepper
2 tsps chopped fresh parsley
Lemon wedges for garnishing (optional)

1. Sift the flour into a deep bowl with a pinch of salt. Gradually stir in the water in the amount needed to make a very thick batter.

2. Heat the oil to 365°, or until it is hot enough to brown a 1-inch cube of bread in 60 seconds, in a large, deep pan. A deep-sided sauté pan is ideal.

3. Take 3 fish at a time and dip them into the batter together. Press their tails together firmly to make a fan shape.

4. Lower them carefully into the oil. Cook in several batches until crisp and golden. Continue in the same way with all the remaining fish.

Step 3 Dip three fish at a time into the batter and when coated press the tails together firmly to form a fan shape.

Step 4 Lower the fish carefully into the hot oil to preserve the shape.

5. Meanwhile, squeeze out the bread and place in a food processor with the garlic and lemon juice. With the processor running, add the oil in a thin, steady stream. Add water if the mixture is too thick and dry. Add salt and pepper and stir in the parsley by hand. When all the fish are cooked, sprinkle lightly with salt and arrange on serving plates with some of the garlic sauce and lemon wedges, if desired.

Cook's Notes

Time
Preparation takes about 30 minutes, cooking takes about 3 minutes per batch for the fish.

Cook's Tip
The fish should be eaten immediately after frying. If it is necessary to keep the fish warm, place them on a wire cooling rack covered with paper towels in a slow oven with the door open. Sprinkling fried food lightly with salt helps to absorb excess fat.

Serving Idea
Serve with thinly-sliced whole-wheat bread and butter for a more substantial first course, or light lunch/supper dish.

ARTICHOKES WITH GARLIC MAYONNAISE

Home-made mayonnaise is in a class by itself, and with the addition of garlic it makes a perfect sauce for artichokes.

4 medium-sized globe artichokes
1 slice lemon
1 bay leaf
Pinch salt

Garlic Mayonnaise
2 egg yolks
2 cloves garlic, crushed
Salt, pepper and lemon juice to taste
1 cup olive oil
Chervil leaves to garnish

1. To prepare the artichokes, break off the stems, twisting to remove any tough fibers. Trim the base so that the artichokes will stand upright. Trim the points from all the leaves and wash the artichokes well. Bring a large saucepan or stock pot full of water to the boil with the slice of lemon and bay leaf. Add a pinch of salt and, when the water is boiling, add the artichokes. Allow to cook for 25 minutes over a moderate heat.

2. Use a whisk to beat the egg yolks and garlic with a pinch of salt and pepper in a deep bowl or use a blender or food processor. Add the olive oil a few drops at a time while whisking by hand, or in a thin steady stream with the machine running. If preparing the sauce by hand, once half the oil is added, the remainder may be added in a thin, steady stream. Add lemon juice once the sauce becomes very thick. When all the oil has been added, adjust the seasoning and add more lemon juice to taste.

3. When the artichokes are cooked, the bottom leaves will pull away easily. Drain upside-down on paper towels or in a colander. Allow to cool and serve with the garlic mayonnaise. Garnish with chervil.

Step 1 Trim the pointed ends from all the leaves of the artichoke.

Step 2 Add the oil to the egg yolks in a thin, steady stream to prevent curdling.

Step 3 Pull away one of the bottom leaves to see if the artichoke is cooked.

Cook's Notes

Time
Preparation will take approximately 30 minutes and cooking approximately 25 minutes.

Cook's Tip
If this sauce or other mayonnaise needs to be thinned for coating, mix with a little hot water. A damp cloth under the mixing bowl will stop it spinning when making mayonnaise by hand.

Serving Idea
To eat, peel the leaves off one at a time and dip the fleshy part of the leaf into the sauce. Work down to the thistle or choke and remove with a teaspoon. Break artichoke bottom into pieces and dip into sauce.

RATATOUILLE

This is probably one of the most familiar dishes from southern
France. Either hot or cold, it's full of the warm sun of Provence.

2 eggplants, halved and scored
4-6 zucchini, depending on size
3-6 tbsps olive oil
2 onions, peeled and thinly sliced
2 green peppers, seeded, sliced and cut into 1-inch
  pieces
1 large clove garlic, crushed
2lb ripe tomatoes, peeled and quartered
2 tsps chopped fresh basil or 1 tsp dried basil
Salt and pepper
½ cup dry white wine

1. Lightly salt the eggplant halves and place on paper
towels to drain for about 30 minutes. Rinse and pat dry.
Slice the eggplant and zucchini thickly and set them aside.

2. Pour 3 tbsps of the olive oil into a large skillet over a
medium heat and when hot, lightly brown the onions, green
peppers and zucchini slices. Remove the vegetables to a
casserole and add the eggplant slices to the skillet. Cook
to brown both sides lightly and place in the casserole with
the other vegetables. Add extra oil as needed while cooking the vegetables.

3. Add the garlic and tomatoes to the oil and cook for
1 minute. Add the garlic and tomatoes to the rest of the
vegetables along with any remaining olive oil in the skillet.
Add basil, salt, pepper and wine and bring to the boil over
moderate heat. Cover and reduce the heat to low, to allow
the vegetables to simmer. If the vegetables need moisture
during cooking, add a little white wine.

4. When the vegetables are tender, remove them from the
casserole to a serving dish and boil any remaining liquid in
the pan rapidly over a high heat to reduce to about 2 tbsps.
Pour over the ratatouille to serve.

Step 1 Score and
salt the eggplants
and leave to drain.

Step 2 Brown all the
vegetables lightly.

Step 3 Combine all
the ingredients and
simmer gently.

Cook's Notes

Time
Leave eggplants to stand
30 minutes while preparing
remaining vegetables. Cook
combined ingredients for
approximately 35 minutes.

Cook's Tip
Vegetables in this stew are
traditionally served quite
soft. If crisper vegetables are
desired, shorten the cooking time but
make sure the eggplant is thoroughly
cooked.

Serving Idea
Accompany with shredded
cheese and good crusty
bread for a light vegetarian meal.

HERBY TOMATOES

A light, delicious appetizer which is perfect served before a
substantial main course.

4 large ripe tomatoes
2 tbsps olive oil
1 clove garlic, crushed
2 slices white bread, crusts removed
1 tbsp chopped parsley
2 tsp chopped thyme or marjoram
Salt and pepper

Step 2 Chop the herbs and bread together until well mixed.

Step 1 Scoop out seeds and juice to create space for the filling.

Step 3 Press the filling into the tomatoes.

1. Cut the tomatoes in half and score the cut surface. Sprinkle with salt and leave upside-down in a colander to drain. Allow the tomatoes to drain for 1-2 hours. Rinse the tomatoes and scoop out most of the juice and pulp.

2. Mix the olive oil and garlic together and brush both sides of the bread with the mixture, leaving it to soften. Chop the herbs and the bread together until well mixed.

3. Press the filling into the tomatoes and sprinkle with any remaining garlic and olive oil mixture.

4. Cook the tomatoes in an ovenproof dish under a pre-heated broiler under low heat for the first 5 minutes. Then raise the dish or the heat to brown the tomatoes on top. Serve immediately.

Cook's Notes

Time
Preparation takes about 15 minutes, tomatoes need 1-2 hours to drain. Cooking takes approximately 5-8 minutes.

Cook's Tip
Can be prepared in advance up to broiling and finished off just before serving.

Serving Idea
Serve as a first course or a side dish. Especially nice with lamb or beef.

FRESH CREAMED MUSHROOMS

For a recipe that has been around since Colonial times,
this one is surprisingly up-to-date.

1lb even-sized button mushrooms
1 tbsp lemon juice
2 tbsps butter or margarine
1 tbsp flour
¼ tsp freshly grated nutmeg
Salt and white pepper
1 small bay leaf
1 blade mace
1 cup heavy cream
1 tbsp dry sherry

Step 2 Cook the flour gently in the butter for about 1 minute.

Step 3 Test with a sharp knife to see if the mushrooms are tender.

Step 1 Trim the mushroom stems level with the caps. Do not use the stems for this recipe.

1. Wash the mushrooms quickly and dry them well. Trim the stems level with the caps. Leave whole if small, halve or quarter if large. Toss with the lemon juice and set aside.

2. In a medium saucepan, melt the butter or margarine over a low heat and stir in the flour. Cook, stirring gently, for about 1 minute. Remove from the heat, add the nutmeg, salt, pepper, bay leaf and mace and gradually stir in the cream.

3. Return the pan to a medium heat and bring to the boil, stirring constantly. Allow to boil for about 1 minute, or until thickened. Reduce the heat to low and add the mushrooms. Simmer gently, covered, for about 5 minutes, or until the mushrooms are tender. Add the sherry during the last few minutes of cooking. Remove bay leaf and blade mace. Sprinkle with additional grated nutmeg before serving.

Cook's Notes

Time
Preparation takes about 20 minutes, and cooking takes about 7 minutes.

Cook's Tip
If the mushrooms are clean, do not wash them. If washing is necessary, rinse them very quickly and pat dry quickly. Mushrooms absorb water easily.

Serving Ideas
Serve on hot toast, or in individual custard cups or scallop shells accompanied with hot buttered toast or melba toast.

GUACAMOLE

This is a popular Mexican dip, usually eaten with chips, savory biscuits, or sticks of raw vegetables, such as cucumber, celery, or carrot.

1 ripe avocado
1 tbsp lemon juice
1 large tomato
1 large clove garlic
1 tsp salt
¼ tsp black pepper
1 tsp olive oil
2-3 sprigs fresh coriander leaves, finely chopped
1 small onion, finely chopped

Step 1 Put the avocado flesh into a bowl and mash it thoroughly with the lemon juice to prevent it discoloring.

Step 1 Peel the avocado.

Step 5 Put the avocado mixture into a blender, or food processor, and blend thoroughly for about 30 seconds, until it is smooth.

1. Peel the avocado and cut the flesh away from the stone. Put the flesh into a bowl and mash it thoroughly with the lemon juice.

2. Cut a small cross into the skin of the tomato with a sharp knife and plunge it into boiling water for 30 seconds. Remove the tomato from the water and peel off the skin. Chop the tomato, removing any woody core, and put this into the bowl with the avocado.

3. Peel the clove of garlic and crush it with the salt.

4. Stir the garlic, pepper, oil and coriander leaves into the avocado.

5. Put the avocado mixture into a blender or food processor, and blend to a smooth pulp.

6. Transfer the avocado mixture to a small bowl and gently stir in the onion.

Cook's Notes

Time
Preparation will take about 5 minutes.

Cook's Tip
Add 1 seeded and finely chopped green chili pepper to the avocado purée, at the same time as the onion, for a spicy variation.

Serving Idea
Serve the dip surrounded by sticks of raw vegetables, such as cucumber, celery, pepper, carrots, or tortilla chips.

AVOCADO MOUSSE

Salads set with gelatin are cooling treats in summer or perfect
do-ahead dishes anytime.

Juice of 1 small lemon
1½ tbsps unflavored gelatin
2 ripe avocados
3oz cream cheese or low fat soft cheese
½ cup sour cream or plain yogurt
2 tbsps mayonnaise (see basic recipes)
3 oranges, peeled and segmented
Flat Italian parsley or coriander to garnish

1. Reserve about 2 tsps of the lemon juice. Pour the rest into a small dish, sprinkle the gelatin on top and allow to stand until spongy.

2. Cut the avocados in half and twist to separate. Reserve half of one avocado with the stone attached, brush the cut surface with lemon juice, wrap in plastic wrap and keep in the refrigerator.

3. Remove the stone from the other half and scrape the pulp from the three halves into a food processor.

4. Add the cheese, sour cream or yogurt and mayonnaise and process until smooth.

5. Melt the gelatin over a low heat and add it to the avocado mixture with the machine running.

6. Place a small disc of wax paper in custard cups, oil the sides of the cups and the paper and pour in the mixture. Tap the cups lightly on a flat surface to smooth the top and eliminate any air bubbles, cover with plastic wrap and chill until set.

Step 6 Pour the avocado mixture into oiled custard cups with a piece of wax paper in the bottom.

Step 7 Make sure the mixture pulls away completely from the sides of the dishes before inverting and shaking to unmold.

7. Loosen the set mixture carefully from the sides of the cups and invert each onto a serving plate to unmold. Peel and slice the remaining avocado half and use to decorate the plate along with the orange segments. Place parsley or coriander leaves on top of each avocado mold to serve.

Cook's Notes

Time
Preparation takes about 25 minutes. The mousses will take about 2 hours to set completely.

Cook's Tip
Adding lemon juice to the mixture and brushing the avocado slices with lemon juice will help to keep them from turning brown. The mousses will discolor slightly even with the addition of lemon juice if kept in the refrigerator more than one day.

Serving Idea
Serve with tortilla chips for a good contrast of flavors and textures.

STUFFED EGGPLANTS

This delicious eggplant dish is highly reminiscent of Andalucia in Spain where tomatoes, rice and tuna fish are very popular ingredients.

4 small eggplants
3¾ tbsps olive oil
1 small onion, finely chopped
1 clove garlic, minced
¾ cup cooked whole-grain rice
7oz can tuna in oil, drained and fish coarsely flaked
1¼ tbsps mayonnaise (see basic recipes)
1¼ tsps curry powder
4 fresh tomatoes, skinned, seeded and chopped
1 tbsp coarsely chopped parsley
Freshly ground black pepper

Step 1 Taking care not to break the skins, score the cut surface of the eggplant halves at regular intervals with a sharp, pointed knife.

Step 4 Carefully scoop the flesh from each cooled eggplant half, without breaking the skin.

1. Cut the eggplants in half lengthwise. Score the cut surfaces lightly with a sharp knife at regular intervals.

2. Brush the scored surface ligthly with 1 tbsp of the olive oil and place the eggplants on a greased baking dish.

3. Bake the eggplants in a preheated oven 375°F, for 15 minutes, or until beginning to soften.

4. Cool the eggplants slightly, then carefully scoop the center flesh from each half. Take care that you do not break the skin at this stage.

5. Cook the chopped onion over a low heat in the remaining olive oil for 3 minutes, or until it is just transparent.

6. Add the garlic and the eggplant flesh, and cook for another 2 minutes. Season to taste with pepper.

7. Add the rice, flaked tuna, mayonnaise, curry powder, tomatoes, parsley and black pepper to the eggplant mixture, and mix together well.

8. Pile equal amounts of this rice and tuna filling into the eggplant shells. Return the filled eggplants to the oven-proof baking dish. Brush with the remaining olive oil, and bake in the oven for another 25 minutes. Serve piping hot.

Cook's Notes

Time
Preparation will take 40 minutes, cooking takes about 50 minutes.

Cook's Tip
Use a serrated grapefruit knife to remove the baked eggplant flesh without tearing the skins.

Serving Idea
Serve with a crisp mixed leaf salad and black olives.

CORN PANCAKES

Cornmeal, either yellow, white or blue, is an important ingredient in Southwestern recipes. Here it's combined with corn in a light and different kind of appetizer.

1 cup yellow cornmeal
1 tbsp flour
1 tsp baking soda
1 tsp salt
2 eggs, separated
2 cups buttermilk
Oil
10oz frozen corn
Red pepper preserves, for garnish
Green onions, chopped, for garnish
Sour cream, for garnish

1. Sift the dry ingredients into a bowl, adding any coarse meal that remains in the sieve.

2. Mix the egg yolks and buttermilk together and gradually beat into the dry ingredients. Cover and leave to stand for at least 15 minutes.

3. Whisk the egg whites until stiff but not dry and fold into the cornmeal mixture.

4. Lightly grease a skillet with oil and drop in about 2 tbsps of batter. Sprinkle with the corn and allow to cook until the underside is golden brown. Turn the pancakes and cook the second side until golden. Continue with the remaining batter and corn. Keep the cooked pancakes warm.

Step 2 Mix the egg yolks and buttermilk and gradually beat into the dry ingredients.

Step 4 Sprinkle the uncooked sides of the pancakes with some of the corn before turning over to cook further.

5. To serve, place three pancakes on warm side plates. Add a spoonful of sour cream and red pepper preserves to each and sprinkle over finely sliced or shredded green onions.

Cook's Notes

Time
Prepration takes about 30 minutes, including standing time for the pancake batter. Cooking takes about 3-4 minutes per pancake.

Cook's Tip
Allowing the pancake batter to stand 15 minutes before using it will produce a batter that is lighter and easier to use. This standing time also helps the cornmeal to soften.

Serving Idea
Serve as an appetizer with the red pepper preserves, sour cream and green onions or serve alone as a side dish to a main course.

SPICY VEGETABLE FRITTERS WITH TOMATO SAUCE

Use any favorite vegetables or those that are in season. The hotness of the sauce can be tempered by using less of the red chili pepper.

1 cup all-purpose flour
1 cup whole-wheat flour
1½ tsps salt
1 tsp chili powder
1½ tsps ground cumin
1¼ cups water
1½ tbsps lemon juice
1 small cauliflower, broken into small flowerets
1 eggplant, cut into 1-inch pieces
3 zucchini, trimmed and cut into 1-inch pieces
2 cups button mushrooms
1 sweet red pepper, seeded and cut into 1-inch squares
1 green pepper, seeded and cut into 1-inch squares
1 large potato, peeled and cut into 1-inch cubes
1⅔ cups canned plum tomatoes, drained
1 red chili pepper, seeded and chopped
1 clove garlic, minced
1 small onion, peeled and finely chopped
1½ tbsps white wine vinegar
1½ tbsps soft brown sugar
Salt and freshly ground black pepper, to taste
1 sliced green chili pepper for garnish
1 sliced red chili pepper for garnish
Oil

1. Put the flours, salt, chili powder and cumin into a large bowl. Make a slight well in the center.

2. Gradually add the water and lemon juice to the flour, beating well until a smooth batter is formed.

3. Wash the fresh vegetables and allow them to drain completely on paper towels or a clean coth.

4. Put the tomatoes, fresh chili, garlic, onions, vinegar and sugar into a food processor or liquidizer and blend until the sauce is smooth.

5. Pour the sauce mixture into a small pan over a low heat and heat gently, stirring until it is completely warmed through. Season with salt, transfer to a small serving dish and garnish with slices of red and green chilies.

6. Heat some vegetable oil in a deep-fat fryer or wok until it is 365°F, or hot enough to brown a 1-inch cube of bread in just under a minute.

7. Make sure the vegetables are completely dry, patting any moisture off them with paper towels if necessary.

8. Using a slotted spoon, drop the vegetables, a few at a time, into the batter and dip them to coat thoroughly.

9. Remove the vegetables from the batter, again using the slotted spoon, and allow some of the batter to drain back into the bowl.

10. Drop the vegetables into the hot oil, and cook quickly until they are golden brown and the batter puffy.

11. Remove the cooked vegetables from the oil and drain completely on paper towels, keeping them warm until all the remaining vegetables have been prepared in this manner.

12. Serve immediately, providing small forks with which to dip the vegetables into the spicy tomato sauce.

Cook's Notes

Time
Preparation takes about 20 minutes, cooking takes about ½ hour.

Cook's Tip
It is important to ensure that the vegetables are completely dry before coating with the batter, or it will not cover them.

Serving Idea
Garnish the sauce with tomato roses (see garnish section) instead of the chili peppers.

STUFFED TOMATOES

Use summer's ripe tomatoes to their best advantage as an
appetizer or side dish with a creamy cheese filling.

4 beefsteak tomatoes
4 anchovy fillets
1 tbsp capers
2 green onions
4oz German Camembert or Bavarian Brie
2 tsps caraway seeds
Salt and freshly ground black pepper

Step 1 Remove the stalk from the top of each tomato. Slice off the bottom of each tomato.

Step 1 Remove the pulp and seeds from the tomatoes with a teaspoon.

Step 2 Soak the anchovies in milk for about 5 minutes to remove the salt.

1. Remove the core from the bottom of each tomato. Cut a slice from the rounded end of each tomato and scoop out the pulp and seeds with a small teaspoon. Strain out the seeds and use the pulp and juice for the filling.

2. Place the anchovies in a little milk and leave to soak for about 5 minutes. Rinse, pat dry and chop. If the capers are large, chop them roughly. Chop the green onions finely and mash with the cheese, capers, anchovies, caraway seeds, salt and pepper. Add the reserved tomato juice and pulp and mix the ingredients together thoroughly.

3. Spoon the filling into the tomatoes and place them on serving plates. Top with the reserved tomato slices and serve chilled.

Cook's Notes

Time
Preparation takes about 15 minutes. Tomatoes should be chilled for at least 30 minutes before serving.

Cook's Tip
If beefsteak tomatoes are not available, substitute 2 ripe tomatoes per person.

Serving Idea
Tomatoes may be served in a vinaigrette dressing. Accompany with brown bread and butter or rolls.

SERVES 4

ENDIVE BAKED WITH HAM & CHEESE

Normally a salad vegetable, chicory or endive can also be
served cooked. This makes a first course or light main dish.

4 large, firm Belgian endive (chicory)
½ cup milk
½ cup cold water
Pinch salt
4 slices cooked ham
4 slices Emmenthal cheese, cut ¼ inch thick
Butter or margarine

Step 2 Cook until
the endive is just
tender to the point of
a knife.

Step 1 Trim the base
of each endive and
remove the central
core using a small,
sharp knife.

Step 3 Wrap each
endive in a slice of
ham and top with a
slice of cheese.

1. Trim the base of the endive and wash well under cold
running water. Using a small, sharp knife, remove the center core at the base.

2. Place the endive in a sauté pan and pour over the milk
and water. Use a pan that just fits the endive snugly. Add a
pinch of salt and heat to simmering. Cover the pan and
cook over a low heat for about 20 minutes or until the endive is tender but not falling apart. Drain on paper towels.

3. Wrap each endive in a slice of ham and place in a well-
buttered ovenproof dish. Place a slice of cheese on top of
each endive roll and bake in a preheated oven at 400°F.

4. Bake for about 10 minutes or until the cheese melts.
Place under a preheated broiler to brown the top, if desired. Serve immediately.

Cook's Notes

 Time
Preparation takes about
20 minutes, cooking takes
about 35 minutes.

Cook's Tip
Once cut, the endive will
begin to turn brown on the
cut surfaces. This does not affect the
taste and in the case of this dish
does not affect the appearance.
Sprinkle with lemon juice to prevent
discoloration.

 Serving Idea
Serve as a first course with
brown bread and butter or
rolls. Garnish with a sweet red
pepper lattice (see garnish section)
before broiling.

SERVES 4

IMPERIAL ASPARAGUS

A special occasion appetizer – a real treat when asparagus is
very tender.

2lbs green asparagus
3 tbsps butter or margarine
3 tbsps flour
1 cup asparagus cooking liquid or chicken stock
½ cup white wine
2 egg yolks
4 tbsps heavy cream
Salt and white pepper
Pinch sugar

Step 2 Cook the asparagus in a sauté pan of boiling salted water. Place all the asparagus tips in one direction and set that part of the pan off the heat.

Step 1 Hold the trimmed asparagus spears in the palm of your hand and take off the outer skin in thin strips using a swivel vegetable peeler.

1. Trim the ends of the asparagus to remove the top parts and to make the spears the same length. Using a swivel vegetable peeler, pare the stalks up to the tips.

2. To cook the asparagus, tie the spears in a bundle and stand them upright in a deep saucepan of lightly salted boiling water. Alternatively, place the spears in a large sauté pan of boiling salted water. If using a sauté pan, place half on and half off the heat, with the tips of the asparagus off the heat.

3. Cook, uncovered, over a low heat for about 12-15 minutes, or until the asparagus is tender. Drain and reserve the cooking liquid. Keep the asparagus warm in a covered serving dish.

4. To prepare the sauce, melt the butter in a heavy-based saucepan over a low heat and stir in the flour off the heat. Gradually beat in the asparagus cooking liquid or chicken stock and add the wine. Stir until the sauce is smooth and then place over a low heat.

5. Bring the sauce to the boil, stirring constantly, and allow to boil for about 1-2 minutes, or until thickened.

6. Beat the egg yolks and cream together and add a few spoonfuls of the hot sauce. Return the egg and cream mixture to the pan, stirring constantly. Reheat if necessary but do not allow the sauce to boil once the egg is added. Add salt and white pepper and a pinch of sugar if desired. Pour over the asparagus to serve.

Cook's Notes

 Time
Preparation takes about 30 minutes, cooking takes about 12-15 minutes for the asparagus and about 10 minutes for the sauce.

 Cook's Tip
Use white asparagus if green is unavailable.

 Serving Idea
Serve as a vegetable side dish with ham and new potatoes or as a first course on its own sprinkled with paprika.

SERVES 6

CARROT AND ZUCCHINI SALAD

This salad couldn't be easier. It is colorful, inexpensive and can be made almost all year round.

12oz carrots, peeled
12oz zucchini, topped and tailed
Grated rind and juice of 2 oranges
3 tbsps olive oil
Salt and pepper
4 tbsps unblanched almonds, chopped

Step 1 Shred the carrots on the coarse side of a grater.

Step 2 Shred the zucchini coarsely and add to the carrots.

Step 3 When grating oranges or other citrus fruit, use a pastry brush to remove all the zest from holes in grater.

1. Shred the carrots on the coarse side of a grater or use the coarse shredding blade of a food processor. Place in a large bowl.

2. Shred the zucchini in the same way and add to the carrots.

3. Grate the orange on the fine side of the grater and then cut in half to squeeze the juice. Mix the juice and rind with the olive oil and salt and pepper. Pour over the carrots and the zucchini and stir well. Leave to marinate for about 15 minutes.

4. Sprinkle over the almonds and toss the salad just before serving.

Cook's Notes

Time
Preparation takes about 15-25 minutes. Vegetables should marinate for about 15 minutes.

Cook's Tip
The salad may be prepared in advance and left to stand longer than 15 minutes. Cover well and refrigerate.

Serving Idea
Serve in individual bowls with a selection of other tapas. Spoon onto lettuce leaves for a first course or serve as a side salad.

ROAST PEPPER SALAD

Charring the peppers makes the skins easier to remove and gives a slightly smoky taste that is very pleasant.

6 sweet red peppers
6 tbsps olive oil
2 tbsps red or white wine vinegar
Salt and pepper
1 clove garlic, roughly chopped
1 green onion, diagonally sliced

Step 2 Flatten the peppers by pushing down with the palm of the hand.

1. Preheat a broiler to medium and cut the peppers in half, removing the seeds, stems and cores.

2. Flatten the peppers with the palm of your hand and brush the skin side of each pepper lightly with oil. Place the peppers under the broiler.

3. Broil the peppers until the skins are well charred on top. Do not turn the peppers over.

4. Wrap the peppers in a clean towel and leave to stand for about 15-20 minutes.

Step 3 Broil the lightly-oiled peppers until the skins are charred.

Step 5 Use a small, sharp knife to peel away the skin.

5. Unwrap the peppers and peel off the skin using a small, sharp knife. Cut the peppers into strips or into 1-inch pieces. Mix the remaining oil with the vinegar, salt and pepper. Place the peppers in a serving dish and pour over the dressing. Sprinkle over the garlic and green onion and leave the peppers to stand for about 30 minutes before serving.

Cook's Notes

Time
Preparation takes about 20 minutes. Broiling time for the peppers is approximately 10-12 minutes.

Cook's Tip
The peppers must be well charred for the skin to loosen easily. Wrapping peppers in a tea towel creates steam, which helps to loosen the skin more easily.

Serving Idea
Serve as a tapa or mix with cooked cold rice for a more substantial salad.

BEAN, TUNA AND TOMATO SALAD

Tuna and tomatoes are two popular ingredients in Italian antipasto dishes. Add beans for an attractive and easy first course or salad.

1lb canned beans, e.g. navy or haricot beans
6oz canned tuna in oil
Chopped fresh herbs (parsley, oregano, basil or marjoram)
Juice of 1 lemon
8 tbsps olive oil
Salt and pepper
6-8 tomatoes, sliced

Step 2 Chop the herbs finely with a large knife using a mixture of different herbs, if desired.

1. Drain the beans, rinse and leave in a colander to dry. Drain the tuna and flake it into a bowl.

2. Chop the herbs finely and mix with lemon juice, oil, salt and pepper. Add the beans to the tuna fish in the bowl and pour over the dressing, tossing carefully. Do not allow the tuna to break up too much.

3. Adjust the seasoning and pile the salad into a mound in a shallow serving dish. Cut the tomatoes into rounds about ¼ inch thick and place against the mound of salad. Serve immediately.

Step 3 Mound the salad in the serving dish and place the tomatoes around it.

Cook's Notes

Time
Preparation takes about 15 minutes.

Cook's Tip
Adding a little finely-minced garlic with the herbs gives the salad extra zest.

Serving Idea
If desired, serve the salad on individual plates lined with radicchio or curly endive.

MUSHROOM SALAD

Mushrooms have a flavor all of their own and do not require salt. This salad can be made using cultivated mushrooms, but it is extra special when prepared with wild ones.

1lb button or oyster mushrooms
1 medium-sized onion
3¾ tbsps vegetable oil
1¼ tbsps freshly chopped parsley
1 cucumber, finely diced
3-4 tomatoes, peeled, seeded and sliced
5 tbsps olive oil
1¼ tbsps white wine vinegar
Freshly ground black pepper
1 small iceberg lettuce

1. Trim the mushrooms and rub clean with a damp cloth.

2. Slice the mushrooms very thinly and chop the onion finely.

Step 2 Slice the mushrooms very thinly with a sharp knife.

3. Heat the vegetable oil in a large skillet over a medium heat and gently sauté the mushrooms and onion for 2-3 minutes, or until they are just soft. Allow to cool.

Step 3 Cook the mushrooms and onion gently in hot oil until they just begin to soften.

Step 4 Add the parsley, cucumber and tomatoes to the mushrooms, mixing well to combine ingredients evenly.

4. When the mushrooms have cooled, stir in the parsley, cucumber and tomatoes.

5. Mix together the oil, vinegar and pepper in a small jug, and pour over all the other ingredients.

6. Stir gently to coat evenly, and chill for at least 2 hours.

7. Shred the lettuce finely and arrange on a serving plate. Spread the chilled mushrooms evenly over the lettuce.

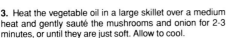

Cook's Notes

Time
Preparation takes 10 minutes, cooking takes 5 minutes. Chilling time is a minimum of 2 hours.

Cook's Tip
The salad can be prepared a day in advance and stored in the refrigerator until required.

Serving Idea
Serve with Melba toast or crusty whole-wheat rolls.

SPRING SALAD

This delicious salad serves as an ideal appetizer, and can be
used as a sandwich spread, too.

12-14oz cottage cheese
1 carrot
8 radishes
2 green onions, thinly sliced
Salt and pepper
1 tsp chopped fresh dill or marjoram
½ cup sour cream or thick plain yogurt
Lettuce leaves (red oak leaf lettuce, curly endive or
    radicchio)

Step 3 Trim the root
ends from the green
onions and any part
of the green tops
that looks damaged.

Step 2 Using the
coarse side of a
grater, shred the
carrots into short
strips.

Step 3 Use a
sharp knife to slice
through both onions
at once to save time.

1. If cottage cheese is very liquidy, pour into a fine strainer
and leave to stand for about 15-20 minutes for some of the
liquid to drain away. Alternatively, cut down on the amount
of sour cream.

2. Peel the carrot and shred using the coarse side of the
grater or the coarse shredding blade in a food processor.
Make sure the carrot is shredded into short strips.

3. Shred the radishes with the grater and cut the onions
into thin rounds with a large, sharp knife.

4. Mix all the ingredients together, except the lettuce
leaves, and chill for about 20 minutes to blend all the
flavors.

5. To serve, place lettuce leaves on individual plates and
mound the cottage cheese salad mixture on top. If desired,
sprinkle with more chopped fresh dill.

Cook's Notes

Time
Preparation takes about
20 minutes and salad
requires 15-20 minutes refrigeration.

Cook's Tip
Add finely chopped sweet
red or green pepper or
cucumber to the salad. If using
cucumber, shred and sprinkle with
salt. Leave to stand 30 minutes, rinse
and pat dry.

Serving Idea
Serve with thinly sliced
whole-wheat or rye bread,
lightly buttered. The salad may also
be served with French bread.

CAESAR SALAD

Both Los Angeles and Tijuana take credit for this salad, said to have been concocted one evening from the only ingredients left in the kitchen.

6 anchovy fillets, soaked in 4 tbsps milk
1 clove garlic, left whole
1 cup olive oil
4 slices French bread, cut into ½-inch cubes
1 egg, cooked 1 minute
Juice of 1 small lemon
Salt and pepper
1 head Romaine lettuce
4 tbsps grated Parmesan cheese

Step 2 Cook the cubes of French bread in the hot oil, stirring them constantly for even browning.

1. Leave the anchovies to soak in the milk for 15 minutes. Rinse and pat dry on paper towels. Chop roughly.

2. Crush the garlic and leave in the oil for about 30 minutes. Heat all but 6 tbsps of the oil in a skillet over a medium heat until hot. Cook the cubes of bread until golden brown, stirring constantly with a metal spoon for even browning. Drain on paper towels.

3. Break the cooked egg into a bowl and beat well with the lemon juice, salt and pepper. Toss the lettuce with the remaining garlic oil and anchovies. Add the egg mixture and toss to coat well. Place in a clean serving bowl and sprinkle over the croûtons and Parmesan cheese. Serve at room temperature.

Step 3 To make the dressing, break the egg into the bowl and mix well with the lemon juice and seasoning until slightly thickened.

Step 3 Add the oil and anchovies to the lettuce separately and then toss with the egg dressing mixture.

Cook's Notes

Time
Preparation takes about 30 minutes and cooking takes about 3-5 minutes for the croûtons.

Cook's Tip
Soaking anchovy fillets in milk before using them neutralizes the strong salty taste.

Serving Idea
Arrange the salad on individual plates and serve with crusty French bread.

GREEN GODDESS SALAD

Californians' love of salads and avocado combine in this fresh
recipe named for its green dressing.

8 anchovy fillets, soaked in milk, rinsed and dried
1 green onion, chopped
2 tbsps chopped fresh tarragon
3 tbsps chopped chives
4 tbsps chopped parsley
1 cup prepared mayonnaise (see basic recipes)
½ cup plain yogurt
2 tbsps tarragon vinegar
Pinch sugar and cayenne pepper
1 large head lettuce
1 avocado, peeled and sliced or cubed
1lb cooked chicken or seafood
1 tbsp lemon juice

1. Combine all the ingredients, except the lettuce, avocado and chicken or seafood and lemon juice in a food processor. Work the ingredients until smooth, well mixed and green. Leave in the refrigerator at least 1 hour for the flavors to blend.

2. Shred the lettuce or tear into bite-sized pieces and arrange on plates.

3. Top the lettuce with the cooked chicken cut into strips or cubes. If using crab or lobster, cut the meat into bite-sized pieces. Shelled shrimp or mussels can be left whole.

4. Spoon the dressing over the chicken or seafood. Brush the avocado slices or toss the cubes with lemon juice and use to garnish the salad. Serve any remaining dressing separately.

Step 1 The dressing should be very well blended and light green after working in a food processor. Alternatively, use a hand blender.

Step 3 Arrange lettuce on individual plates and top with chicken or seafood.

Cook's Notes

Time
Preparation takes about 20 minutes plus at least 1 hour's chilling time for the dressing.

Cook's Tip
Dressing may be prepared ahead of time and kept in the refrigerator for a day or two.

Serving Idea
The dressing may be served as a dip for vegetable crudités or with a tossed salad.

CHINA BEACH SALAD

Named for a stretch of beach near San Francisco, this recipe
reflects the Chinese heritage in California's past and its
present passion for salads.

1lb cooked, peeled shrimp
1lb seedless white grapes, halved if large
6 sticks celery, thinly sliced on diagonal
4oz toasted flaked almonds
4oz canned water chestnuts, sliced or diced
8oz canned litchis or 12oz fresh litchis, peeled
1 small fresh pineapple, peeled, cored and cut into pieces
Chinese cabbage or Belgian endive (chicory)
1½ cups mayonnaise (see basic recipes)
1 tbsp honey
1 tbsp light soy sauce
2 tbsps mild curry powder
Juice of half a lime

Step 1 Trim the point of each quarter of pineapple to remove the core.

1. Combine the shrimp, grapes, celery, almonds, water chestnuts and litchis in a large bowl. Trim off the top and bottom of the pineapple and quarter. Slice off the points of each quarter to remove the core.

2. Slice the pineapple skin away and cut the flesh into bite-size pieces. Add to the shrimp and toss to mix.

Step 2 Use a serrated fruit knife to slice between the skin and pineapple flesh.

3. Break the Chinese cabbage or endive and wash them well. If using Chinese cabbage, shred the leafy part finely, saving the thicker ends of the leaves for other use. Place the Chinese cabbage on salad plates. Separate chicory leaves and arrange them whole. Mix the remaining dressing ingredients thoroughly. Pile the salad ingredients onto the leaves and spoon over some of the dressing, leaving the ingredients showing. Serve remaining dressing separately.

Step 2 Add pineapple pieces to the shrimp and mix well.

Cook's Notes

Time
Preparation takes about 30 minutes.

Cook's Tip
Other seafood may be substituted for the shrimp. Use crab, lobster or shellfish such as mussels.

Serving Idea
Serve in larger quantities as a main course salad for lunch or a light dinner.

CRAB LOUIS

This salad is legendary on Fisherman's Wharf in San Francisco. Once tasted, it is sure to become a favorite.

2 large cooked crabs
1 head iceberg lettuce
4 large tomatoes
4 hard-cooked eggs
1 cup prepared mayonnaise (see basic recipes)
4 tbsps whipping cream
4 tbsps chili sauce or tomato chutney
½ green pepper, seeded and finely diced
3 green onions, finely chopped
Salt and pepper
16 black olives

Step 1 Turn crabs over and press up with thumbs to separate the under-body from the shell.

1. To prepare the crabs, break off the claws and set them aside. Turn the crabs over and press up with thumbs to separate the body from the shell of each.

2. Cut the body into quarters and use a skewer to pick out the white meat. Discard the stomach sac and the lungs (dead-man's fingers). Scrape out the brown meat from the shell to use, if desired.

3. Crack the large claws and legs and remove the meat. Break into shreds, discarding any shell or cartilage. Combine all the meat and set it aside.

4. Shred the lettuce finely, quarter the tomatoes and chop the eggs.

5. Combine the mayonnaise, cream, chili sauce or chutney, green pepper and green onions and mix well.

6. Arrange the shredded lettuce on serving plates and divide the crab meat evenly between them.

7. Spoon some of the dressing over each serving of crab and sprinkle with the chopped egg. Garnish each serving with tomato wedges and olives and serve the remaining dressing separately.

Cook's Notes

Time
Preparation takes about 30-40 minutes.

Cook's Tip
To shred lettuce finely, break off the leaves and stack them up a few at a time. Use a large, sharp knife to cut across the leaves into thin shreds.

Serving Idea
This dish would also serve four as a main course with the addition of vegetables or salad and bread.

TOMATO AND ORANGE SALAD WITH MOZZARELLA AND BASIL

Juicy tomatoes combine with mozzarella and basil in this
classic Italian salad given Californian flair with bright oranges.

4 large tomatoes
4 small oranges
8oz Mozzarella cheese
8 fresh basil leaves
4 tbsps olive oil
1 tbsp balsamic vinegar
Salt and pepper

Step 3 Arrange the ingredients in overlapping circles.

Step 2 Peel the oranges in thin strips to help preserve the round shape of the fruit.

Step 4 Use scissors to finely shred the basil leaves over the top of the salad.

1. Remove the cores from the tomatoes and slice into rounds about ¼ inch thick.

2. Cut a slice from the top and bottom of each orange and, using a serrated fruit knife, remove the peel in thin strips. Make sure to cut off all the white pith. Slice oranges into ¼-inch rounds. Slice the Mozzarella cheese to the same thickness.

3. Arrange the tomatoes, oranges and Mozzarella in overlapping circles, alternating each ingredient.

4. Use scissors to shred the basil leaves finely, and sprinkle over the salad.

5. Mix the remaining ingredients together well and spoon over the salad. Chill briefly before serving.

Cook's Notes

Time
Preparation takes about 20-25 minutes.

Cook's Tip
Shred the basil leaves just before serving, since they tend to turn black if cut and left to stand.

Serving Idea
Tomato roses (see garnish section) could also be used to garnish this dish.

APPETIZERS

Garnishing appetizers is particularly important, as it sets the tone for the rest of the meal, delighting the eye and the palate. Arranging the food attractively is part of the process, but the addition of an extra garnish provides the finishing touch.

ANCHOVY LATTICE

Soak the anchovy fillets in milk for 15 minutes to remove excess salt. Rinse the fillets well in cold water and dry on paper towels. Cut the fillets lengthwise into thin strips. Arrange the strips diagonally over the food. Arrange further strips diagonally in the opposite direction to form a diamond pattern. This may also be done with skinned sweet red peppers and tomatoes.

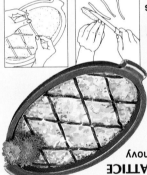

CITRUS BASKETS

The simplest way of using citrus fruits to garnish a dish is to cut them into slices or wedges. However, for special occasions, use lemons, limes or small oranges to make citrus baskets. Firstly, trim the base of the fruit so that it stands up. Mark a ½-inch-wide strip from the middle of the fruit on one side, over the top to the middle of the fruit on the opposite side. This will form the handle. Carefully cut horizontally through from the side of the fruit to the basket

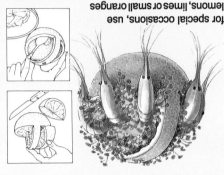

RADISH ROSES

Remove the stalk. Using a sharp knife, cut semicircular petal shapes around the radish, keeping them joined at the base. Cut a second row of petals above the first row, and continue the process until you reach the top of the radish. Place in iced water to allow the petals to open.

RADISH WATER-LILIES

These can be made in the same way as for the tomato version, below. Alternatively, remove the stalk and, using a sharp knife, cut through from the top of the radish four to six times, making sure that the radish remains in one piece at the base. Place the radish water-lily in iced water for 1-2 hours until it has opened out.

TOMATOES

Tomatoes add color to a dish and are also versatile as regards presentation, the most simple method being to cut them into quarters.

handle on both sides and remove both wedges. Scoop out the flesh from under the handle and from the inside of the

basket using a serrated knife. Fill the basket with watercress, shrimp or fresh flowers.

CROÛTONS

Cut bread into small cubes or pretty shapes, using metal cutters, and then brown them lightly in oil, before arranging attractively over soups. For a change, croûtons can be flavored with garlic, which is peeled and fried in the oil before the bread. Alternative

garnishes for soups include toasted nuts, crumbled cooked bacon, or fresh herbs, if available.

FRESH OR SOUR CREAM OR CRÈME FRAÎCHE

Any of the above may be swirled or "feathered" onto the surface of soup for a special touch. To feather use the point of a skewer to draw the cream over the surface of the soup, thus resembling a feather.

TOMATO ROSES

These make a spectacular garnish for special occasions. Choose firm tomatoes, otherwise it is difficult to remove the skin. Using a sharp knife, carefully remove the skin from around

the tomato in a continuous strip about ½-inch wide. Start to curl the skin from the bottom end, with the flesh side inside, forming the center of the flower between the fingers. Continue winding the strip of skin into a rose, making sure that it is not too tight, but tight enough to hold together when used to garnish a dish.

Lemons, radishes and other round fruit or vegetables can also be skinned to make "roses."

TOMATO WATER-LILIES

These make an attractive addition to simple dishes. Remove the stalk. Holding the tomato firmly between

the thumb and forefinger, use a sharp knife to make a zig-zag cut around the middle of the tomato, ensuring that the cut goes through to the center. Carefully separate the tomato halves and use them to garnish cold meats, salamis, salads and other cold dishes.

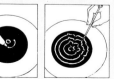

MAIN COURSES

CONTENTS

TROUT MEUNIERE WITH HERBS

The miller (meunier) caught trout fresh from the mill stream
and his wife used the flour which was on hand to dredge them
with, or so the story goes.

4 even-sized trout, cleaned and trimmed
Flour
Salt and pepper
½ cup butter
Juice of 1 lemon
2 tbsps chopped fresh herbs such as parsley, chervil,
   tarragon, thyme or marjoram
Lemon wedges or cones, to garnish

Step 1 Trim the trout tails with scissors to make them neater.

1. Trim the trout tails to make them more pointed. Rinse the trout well.

2. Dredge the trout with flour and shake off the excess. Season with salt and pepper. Heat half the butter in a very large sauté pan over a medium heat and, when foaming, place in the trout. It may be necessary to cook the trout in two batches to avoid overcrowding the pan.

Step 2 Coat trout in flour, shaking off excess.

3. Cook on both sides to brown evenly. Depending on size, the trout should take 5-8 minutes per side to cook. The dorsal fin will pull out easily when the trout are cooked. Remove the trout to a serving dish and keep them warm.

4. Wipe out the pan and add the remaining butter. Cook over a medium heat until beginning to brown, then add the lemon juice and herbs. When the lemon juice is added, the butter will bubble up and sizzle. Pour immediately over the fish and serve garnished with lemon wedges or cones.

Step 3 Brown the trout on both sides. Dorsal fin will pull out easily when done.

Cook's Notes

Time
Preparation takes 15-20 minutes, cooking takes 5-8 minutes per side for the fish and about 5 minutes to brown the butter.

Cook's Tip
If trout is coated in flour too soon before cooking it will become soggy.

Serving Idea
Serve with new potatoes and peeled, cubed cucumber quickly sautéed in butter and chopped dill.

MONKFISH AND PEPPER KEBABS WITH BEARNAISE BUTTER SAUCE

Monkfish is a firm, succulent whitefish, ideal for kebabs.

8 strips bacon, bone and rind removed
2 pieces lemon grass
2lbs monkfish, cut into 2-inch pieces
1 green pepper, seeded, sliced and cut into 2-inch pieces
1 sweet red pepper, seeded, sliced and cut into 2-inch pieces
12 button mushrooms, washed and trimmed
8 bay leaves
Oil for brushing
½ cup dry white wine
4 tbsps tarragon vinegar
2 shallots, finely chopped
1 tbsp chopped fresh tarragon
1 tbsp chopped fresh chervil or parsley
1 cup butter, melted
Salt and pepper

Step 2 Place a piece of fish onto a strip of bacon and top with a shred of lemon grass. Roll and thread onto kebab skewers.

Step 5 Stir the herbs into the reduced wine mixture. Lower the heat and beat in the butter, bit by bit, until the sauce is thick and creamy.

1. Cut the bacon in half lengthways and then in half across. Peel the lemon grass and use only the core. Cut this into small shreds.

2. Place a piece of fish on each strip of bacon and top with a shred of lemon grass. Roll up the bacon around the fish. Thread each fish and bacon roll onto kebab skewers, alternating with the peppers, mushrooms and bay leaves. Brush well with oil.

3. Cook under a moderate broiler for 15 minutes, turning frequently and brushing with more oil, if necessary, until the fish is cooked.

4. Heat together the wine, vinegar and shallots in a small saucepan over a high heat until they are boiling. Cook rapidly until reduced by half.

5. Stir in the herbs and lower the heat to low. Beat in the butter, a little at a time, until the sauce is the thickness of an Hollandaise. Season to taste and serve with the kebabs.

Cook's Notes

Time
Preparation takes about 30 minutes, and cooking takes about 25 minutes.

Cook's Tip
These kebabs are ideal for cooking over a barbecue.

Serving Idea
Serve with a large mixed salad and rice, or pasta.

CHILLED FISH CURRY

This sophisticated, mild curry will serve four as a refreshing
summer lunch, or eight as an elegant appetizer.

8oz fresh salmon fillet
12oz cod fillets
Chicken stock
Salt and pepper
½ cup mayonnaise (see basic recipes)
2 cups plain yogurt
2 tsps curry powder
Juice and grated rind of ½ lemon
¾ cup peeled shrimp

Garnish
Kiwi fruit, peeled and sliced
Sprigs fresh mint
Flaked coconut

1. Put the salmon and cod fillets into a shallow pan and
add just enough chicken stock to cover.

2. Season to taste, bring to the boil, then reduce the heat
to low and simmer, until the fish is just tender.

3. Remove the fish carefully from the cooking liquor and
leave to cool slightly.

4. In a medium-sized bowl, mix together the mayonnaise
and the yogurt. Blend in the curry powder and the lemon
juice and rind.

5. Flake the cooked fish, removing any bones and skin.
Mix the flaked fish into the curry sauce, together with the
shrimp.

6. Arrange the fish curry on serving plates and garnish
with slices of kiwi fruit, sprigs of fresh mint and coconut
flakes.

Step 4 Blend the
curry powder and
the lemon juice and
rind thoroughly into
the mayonnaise and
yogurt mixture.

Step 1 Put the
salmon and cod
fillets into a shallow
pan and pour over
just enough chicken
stock to cover.

Step 5 Flake the
cooked fish, making
sure that all skin and
bones are removed.

Cook's Notes

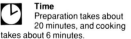

Time
Preparation takes about
20 minutes, and cooking
takes about 6 minutes.

Cook's Tip
If you prefer, use slices of
peeled cucumber instead of
the kiwi fruit.

Serving Idea
Serve with boiled new
potatoes or rice and a crisp
mixed salad.

FISH, ZUCCHINI AND LEMON KEBABS

Ask your fishmonger to fillet and skin the sole for you, if you
feel that you cannot do it yourself.

16 small, thin sole fillets, or 8 larger ones, skinned and cut in half lengthwise
4 tbsps olive oil
1 clove garlic, crushed
Juice ½ lemon
Finely grated rind ½ lemon
Salt and pepper
3 drops Tabasco sauce
2 medium-sized zucchini, cut into ¼-inch slices
1 green pepper, halved, seeded and cut into 1-inch pieces

1. Roll up each sole fillet like a jelly roll and secure with a wooden pick.

2. Place the fish rolls in a shallow dish. Mix together the olive oil, garlic, lemon juice, lemon rind, salt and pepper and Tabasco sauce.

3. Spoon the olive oil mixture evenly over the fish rolls, and chill for about 2 hours.

4. Remove the wooden picks, and carefully thread the rolled fish fillets onto kebab skewers alternately with the zucchini slices and pieces of green pepper.

5. Brush each threaded kebab with a little of the lemon and oil marinade.

6. Arrange the kebab skewers on a broiler pan and cook under a moderately hot broiler for about 8 minutes, carefully turning the kebabs once or twice during cooking and brushing them with a little of the remaining marinade, if required.

Step 1 Roll up each sole fillet like a jelly roll, from the narrow end, and secure each roll with a wooden pick.

Step 4 Thread the rolled fish fillets onto kebab skewers alternately with the zucchini slices and pieces of green pepper.

 Cook's Notes

 Time
Preparation takes about 30 minutes, plus 2 hours chilling time, and cooking takes about 8 minutes.

 Cook's Tip
The marinade ingredients are delicious used with other types of fish.

Serving Idea
Serve the kebabs on a bed of brown rice, sprinkled with chopped parsley.

LAKE TROUT WITH SPINACH AND WALNUT STUFFING

2½ lb lake trout, cleaned
2lbs fresh spinach
1 small onion, finely chopped
¼ cup margarine
½ cup walnuts, roughly chopped
2 cups fresh white bread crumbs
1½ tbsps fresh chopped parsley
1½ tbsps fresh chopped thyme
Pinch grated nutmeg
Salt and pepper
Juice 2 lemons
Watercress sprigs and lemon slices, to garnish

1. Carefully cut the underside of the fish from the end of the slit made when the fish was cleaned, to the tip of the tail.

2. Place the fish, belly side down, on a flat work surface, spreading the cut underside out to balance the fish more easily.

3. Using the palm of your hand, press down along the backbone of the fish, pushing the spine downwards towards the work surface.

4. Turn the fish over and, using a sharp knife, carefully pull the backbone away from the fish, cutting it away with scissors at the base of the head and tail.

5. Remove the backbone completely and pull out any loose bones you may find with a pair of tweezers. Lay the boned fish in the center of a large square of lightly oiled aluminum foil and set aside.

6. Wash the spinach leaves well and tear off any coarse stalks. Put the spinach into a large saucepan and sprinkle with salt. Do not add any extra water. Cover and cook over a moderate heat for about 3 minutes.

7. Turn the spinach into a colander and drain well, pressing with the back of a wooden spoon to remove all the excess moisture.

8. Chop the cooked spinach very finely using a sharp knife.

9. Cook the onion over a low heat in about 1 tbsp of the margarine until soft, but not colored.

10. Stir the cooked onion into the chopped spinach along with the walnuts, bread crumbs, herbs, nutmeg, salt, pepper and half of the lemon juice. Mix well to blend evenly.

11. Use the spinach stuffing to fill the cavity inside the trout. Push the stuffing in firmly, re-shaping the fish as you do so. Allow a little of the stuffing to show between the cut edge of the fish.

12. Seal the foil over the top of the fish, but do not wrap it too tightly.

13. Place the fish in a roasting pan and bake in a preheated oven at 350°F for 35 minutes.

14. Carefully unwrap the fish and transfer it to a large serving dish.

15. Using a sharp knife, peel away the skin from all exposed sides of the fish. If possible, remove some skin from the underside also.

16. While the fish is still hot, dot with the remaining margarine, sprinkle with the remaining lemon juice, then serve garnished with the watercress and sliced lemon.

Cook's Notes

Time
Preparation takes 35-40 minutes, cooking takes about 40 minutes.

Cook's Tip
If you feel that you cannot bone the fish yourself, ask your fishmonger to do it for you, but explain that you wish the bone to be removed from the underside of the fish.

Serving Idea
Serve with potatoes and broiled tomatoes.

SERVES 6

SZECHUAN FISH

This is a hot and spicy dish. The piquant spiciness of
Szechuan pepper is quite different from that of black or white
pepper. Beware, though – too much can numb the mouth temporarily!

Chili peppers, to garnish
1lb halibut fillets
Salt and pepper
1 egg
5 tbsps flour
6 tbsps white wine
Oil
2oz cooked ham, cut in small dice
1-inch piece fresh ginger, finely diced
½-1 red or green chili pepper, cored, seeded and finely
   diced
6 water chestnuts, finely diced
4 green onions, finely chopped
3 tbsps light soy sauce
1 tsp cider vinegar or rice wine vinegar
½ tsp ground Szechuan pepper (optional)
1 cup light stock
1 tbsp cornstarch dissolved in 2 tbsps water
2 tsps sugar

Step 1 Cut the tip of each chili pepper into strips.

Step 3 Allow to soak 4 hours or overnight to open up.

1. To prepare the garnish, choose unblemished chili peppers with the stems on. Using a small, sharp knife, cut the peppers in strips, starting from the pointed end.

2. Cut down to within ½ inch of the stem end. Rinse out the seeds under cold running water and place the peppers in iced water.

3. Leave the peppers to soak for at least 4 hours or overnight until they open up like flowers.

4. Cut the fish into 2-inch pieces and season with salt and pepper. Beat the egg well and add flour and wine to make a batter. Dredge the fish lightly with flour and then dip into the batter.

5. Heat a wok over a medium heat and when hot, add enough oil to deep-fry the fish. When the oil is at 365°F, or hot enough to brown a 1-inch cube of bread in 60 seconds, cook a few pieces of fish at a time, until golden brown. Drain and proceed until all the fish is cooked.

6. Remove all but 1 tbsp of oil from the wok and add the ham, ginger, diced chili pepper, water chestnuts and green onions. Cook for about 1 minute and add the soy sauce and vinegar. If using Szechuan pepper, add at this point. Stir well and cook for a further 1 minute. Remove the vegetables from the pan and set them aside.

7. Add the stock to the wok and bring to the boil. When boiling, add 1 spoonful of the hot stock to the cornstarch mixture. Add the mixture to the stock and reboil, stirring constantly until thickened.

8. Stir in the sugar and return the fish and vegetables to the sauce. Heat through for 30 seconds and serve at once.

Cook's Notes

Time
Preparation takes about 30 minutes. Chili pepper garnish takes at least 4 hours to soak. Cooking takes about 10 minutes.

Cook's Tip
Szechuan peppercorns are available in Chinese supermarkets or delicatessens. If not available, substitute extra chili pepper.

Serving Idea
Serve with plain or fried rice. Do not eat the chili pepper garnish.

6

KUNG PAO SHRIMP WITH CASHEW NUTS

It is said that Kung Pao invented this dish, but to this day no one knows who he was!

½ tsp chopped fresh ginger
1 tsp chopped garlic
1½ tbsps cornstarch
¼ tsp bicarbonate of soda
Salt and pepper
¼ tsp sugar
1lb uncooked shrimp
4 tbsps oil
1 small onion, cut into dice
1 large or 2 small zucchini, cut into ½-inch cubes
1 small sweet red pepper, cut into ½-inch squares
½ cup cashew nuts

Sauce
¾ cup chicken stock
1 tbsp cornstarch
2 tsps chili sauce
2 tsps bean paste (optional)
2 tsps sesame oil
1 tbsp dry sherry or rice wine

1. Mix together the ginger, garlic, cornstarch, bicarbonate of soda, salt, pepper and sugar.

2. Peel the shrimp and remove the dark vein running along the rounded side. If large, cut in half. Place in the dry ingredients, mix well and leave to stand for 20 minutes.

3. Heat the oil in a wok over a high heat and when hot add the shrimp. Cook, stirring, for about 20 seconds, or just until the shrimp change color. Transfer to a plate.

4. Add the onion to the same oil in the wok and cook for about 1 minute. Add the zucchini and sweet red pepper and cook for about 30 seconds.

5. Mix the sauce ingredients together and add to the wok. Cook over a medium heat, stirring constantly, until the sauce is slightly thickened. Add the shrimp and the cashew nuts and heat through completely.

Step 4 To dice the zucchini quickly, top and tail and cut into ½-inch strips.

Step 4 Cut the strips across with a large sharp knife into ½-inch pieces.

Cook's Notes

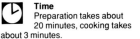 **Time**
Preparation takes about 20 minutes, cooking takes about 3 minutes.

Cook's Tip
If using cooked shrimp, add with the vegetables. Vary the amount of chili sauce to suit your taste.

 Serving Idea
Serve with plain or fried rice.

BOSTON SCROD

Scrod, or baby codfish, provides the perfect base for a
crunchy, slightly spicy topping. Boston is justly famous for it.

4 even-sized cod fillets
Salt and pepper
⅓ cup butter, melted
¾ cup dry bread crumbs
1 tsp dry mustard
1 tsp onion salt
Dash Worcestershire sauce and Tabasco
2 tbsps lemon juice
1 tbsp finely chopped parsley

Step 3 Press the crumbs gently to pack them into place using a spoon or your hand.

Step 1 Season the fish lightly with salt and pepper and brush with some of the melted butter. Broil to pre-cook, but do not brown.

1. Season the fish fillets with salt and pepper and place them on a broiler tray. Brush with butter and broil under a high heat for about 5 minutes.

2. Combine remaining butter with bread crumbs, mustard, onion salt, Worcestershire sauce, Tabasco, lemon juice and parsley.

3. Spoon the mixture carefully on top of each fish fillet, covering it completely. Press down lightly to pack the crumbs into place. Broil for a further 5-7 minutes, or until the top is lightly browned and the fish flakes.

Cook's Notes

Time
Preparation takes about 15 minutes and cooking takes about 12 minutes.

Cook's Tip
The bread crumb topping may be used on other fish such as haddock, halibut or sole.

Serving Idea
Serve with French fries and broccoli.

WHOLE BAKED FISH WITH NEW ENGLAND STUFFING

A whole fish, perfectly cooked, never fails to impress. With an oyster stuffing, it is grand enough for an important dinner party.

4¼-lb fish, cleaned and boned (e g , salmon, or lake trout)

Stuffing
8oz savory cracker crumbs
¼ cup butter, melted
Salt and pepper
2 tsps lemon juice
¼ tsp each dried thyme, sage and marjoram
1 shallot, finely chopped
10 oysters, shelled
Lemon slices, to garnish

Step 3 Spoon the stuffing into the cavity of the fish.

Step 4 Pat the fish to distribute the stuffing evenly.

Step 2 Place the prepared fish on lightly-greased foil, shiny side up.

1. Have the fishmonger clean and bone the fish, leaving on the head and tail. Rinse the fish inside and pat dry.

2. Place the fish on lightly oiled foil. Combine all the stuffing ingredients, mixing so that the oysters do not fall apart.

3. Open the cavity of the fish and spoon in the stuffing.

4. Close the fish and pat out gently so that the stuffing is evenly distributed. Close the foil loosely around the fish and place it directly on the oven shelf or in a large roasting pan. Cook at 400°F for about 40 minutes. Unwrap the fish and place it on a serving plate. Peel off the top layer of skin if desired and garnish with lemon slices.

Cook's Notes

Time
Preparation takes about 25 minutes and cooking takes about 40 minutes.

Serving Idea
Garnish more elaborately with citrus baskets and sprigs of fresh herbs for a dinner party.

Cook's Tip
If asked, the fishmonger will clean and bone the fish for you. Fish may also be stuffed with the bone in, but this makes it more difficult to serve.

SERVES 4

BOILED MAINE LOBSTER

With today's lobster prices, it's hard to imagine that American colonists considered this delectable seafood humble and ordinary.

Salt or seaweed
4 1-lb live lobsters
Lemon wedges
Parsley sprigs
1 cup melted butter

Separate body from tail by arching the lobster backwards. Break off the flipper and push the tail meat out with a fork.

Once the claws are removed from the lobster by twisting off, crack each claw with a nutcracker, hammer or special lobster cracking tool.

Remove the back from the body and discard the stomach sac and lungs. Retain the tomalley or liver to eat, if desired, and crack open the body to extract any remaining meat.

1. Fill a large stock pot full of water and add salt or a piece of seaweed. Bring the water to the boil and then turn off the heat.

2. Place the live lobsters into the pot, keeping your hand well away from the claws. Lower them in claws first.

3. Bring the water slowly back to the boil over a low heat and cook the lobsters for about 15 minutes, or until they turn bright red.

4. Remove lobsters from the water and drain briefly on paper towels. Place on a plate and garnish the plate with lemon wedges and parsley sprigs. Serve with individual dishes of melted butter for dipping.

Cook's Notes

Time
Allow about 20 minutes for the water to boil, and 15 minutes for cooking the lobster.

Cook's Tip
Lobster may be cooked in this way for a variety of recipes that are based on pre-cooked lobster.

Serving Idea
Home-made mayonnaise (see basic recipes) is also good for dipping the lobster.

SNAPPER WITH FENNEL AND ORANGE SALAD

Red snapper brings Florida to mind. Combined with oranges,
it makes a lovely summer meal.

4 even-sized red snapper, cleaned, heads and tails on
Oil for brushing
Juice of 1 lemon
2 heads fennel
2 oranges
3 tbsps light salad oil
Salt and pepper
Pinch sugar, optional

4. Add lemon juice to any orange juice collected in the bowl. Add the salad oil, salt, pepper and a pinch of sugar, if necessary. Mix well and add the fennel, green herb tops and orange segments, stirring carefully.

5. Broil the fish under a medium heat 3-5 minutes per side, depending on thickness. Serve the fish with the heads and tails on, accompanied by the salad.

Step 1 Make three cuts in the side of each fish for even cooking.

Step 2 Slice the fennel in half and remove the cores.

Step 3 Peel and segment the oranges over a bowl to catch the juice.

1. Brush both sides of the fish with oil and cut three slits in the sides of each. Sprinkle with a little of the lemon juice, reserving the rest.

2. Slice the fennel in half and remove the cores. Slice thinly. Also slice the green tops and chop the feathery herb to use in the dressing.

3. Peel the oranges, removing all the white pith, then cut into segments. Peel and segment over a bowl to catch the juice.

Cook's Notes

Time
Preparation takes about 30 minutes and cooking takes about 6-10 minutes.

Cook's Tip
When broiling whole fish, making several cuts on the side of each fish will help to cook it quickly and evenly throughout.

Serving Idea
French bread is good for mopping up the salad juices.

SWORDFISH WITH GRAPEFRUIT TEQUILA SALSA

Rich and dense in texture, swordfish takes very well to a tart
grapefruit accompaniment with a dash of tequila.

4-6 ruby or pink grapefruit (depending on size)
2 limes
½ mild green chili pepper, seeded and finely diced
1 green onion, finely chopped
2 tbsps chopped fresh coriander
1 tbsp sugar
3 tbsps tequila
4-8 swordfish steaks (depending on size)
2 tbsps oil
Black pepper to taste
Coriander sprigs for garnish

1. Remove the zest from the grapefruit and 1 lime with a zester and set it aside.

2. Remove all the pith from the grapefruit and segment them. Squeeze the limes for juice. Mix the grapefruit and citrus zests with the chili pepper, green onion, coriander, sugar, tequila and half the lime juice and set aside.

3. Mix remaining lime juice, oil and pepper together and brush both sides of the fish. Place under a preheated hot broiler and cook for about 4 minutes each side depending on distance from the heat source.

4. To serve, place a coriander sprig on each fish steak and serve with the grapefruit salsa.

Step 1 Remove the zest from the grapefruit with a zester.

Step 2 Use a serrated fruit knife to remove all the pith from the grapefruit.

Cook's Notes

Time
Preparation takes about 35 minutes and cooking takes about 4-6 minutes.

Cook's Tip
For extra flavor, the swordfish steaks may be marinated in a lime juice and oil mixture for up to 1 hour.

Serving Idea
Serve with a mixed salad for a light, healthy supper or lunch dish.

SKATE WINGS WITH BUTTER SAUCE

Fish of any kind is an excellent source of iodine for people
who are on a low salt diet.

4 wings of skate, or 8 thin fish fillets
1 very small onion, sliced
2 parsley stalks
6 black peppercorns
1¼ cups vegetable or fish stock
5 tbsps unsalted butter
1¼ tbsps capers
2½ tbsps white wine vinegar
1¼ tbsps fresh chopped parsley

1. Place the skate wings in one layer in a large deep sauté pan or skillet.

2. Add the onion slices, parsley stalks and peppercorns, then pour over the stock.

3. Bring the fish gently to the boil over a low heat with the pan uncovered and allow to simmer for 10-15 minutes.

4. Carefully remove the skate wings from the pan and arrange on a serving dish.

5. Remove any skin or large pieces of bone, taking great care not to break up the fish. Keep warm.

6. Place the butter into a small pan and cook over a high heat until it begins to brown.

7. Add the capers and immediately remove the butter from the heat. Stir in the vinegar to foam the hot butter.

8. Pour the hot butter sauce over the skate wings and sprinkle with some chopped parsley. Serve immediately.

Step 5 Carefully remove any skin or large bones from the cooked fish using a small sharp pointed knife.

Step 1 Place the skate wings in a pan along with the onion slices, parsley stalks, peppercorns and stock.

Step 7 Add the vinegar to the hot butter and capers. This will cause the butter to foam.

Cook's Notes

Time
Preparation takes 10-15 minutes, cooking will take 20 minutes.

Cook's Tip
When the skate is completely cooked, the meat will pull away from the bones in long strips.

Serving Idea
Serve with boiled new potatoes and a lightly cooked green vegetable.

TARRAGON GRILLED RED SNAPPER

Red snapper is a very decorative little fish that is now readily
available at fishmongers and supermarkets.

4 large or 8 small red snapper, cleaned, scaled, washed
and dried
4 or 8 sprigs of fresh tarragon
5 tbsps vegetable oil
2½ tbsps tarragon vinegar
Salt and pepper
1 egg
1¼ tsps Dijon mustard
½ cup sunflower oil
1¼ tbsps wine vinegar
1¼ tsps brandy
1¼ tbsps chopped fresh tarragon
1¼ tbsps chopped fresh parsley
1¼ tbsps heavy cream
Sprigs of fresh tarragon, to garnish (optional)

1. Rub the inside of each fish with a teaspoonful of salt,
scrubbing hard to remove any discolored membranes inside. Rinse thoroughly.

2. Place a sprig of fresh tarragon inside each fish.

3. Using a sharp knife, cut 2 diagonal slits on the side of
each fish.

4. Mix together the vegetable oil, tarragon vinegar and a
little salt and pepper in a small bowl.

5. Arrange the fish on a shallow dish and pour over the
tarragon/vinegar marinade, brushing some of the mixture
into the cuts on the side of the fish. Refrigerate for
30 minutes.

6. Put the egg into a blender or food processor along with
the mustard and a little salt and pepper. Process for
2-3 seconds to mix.

7. With the machine running, add the oil through the funnel
in a thin, steady stream. Continue blending the dressing
until it is thick and creamy.

8. Add the vinegar, brandy and herbs, and process for a
further 30 seconds to mix well.

9. Lightly beat the cream with a small egg beater until it
thickens.

10. Fold the slightly thickened cream carefully into the oil
and vinegar dressing. Pour into a serving jug and refrigerate until ready to use.

11. Arrange the fish on a broiler pan and cook under a preheated hot broiler for 5-8 minutes per side, depending on
the size of the fish. Baste frequently with the marinade
while cooking, then serve with the sauce and some sprigs
of fresh tarragon.

Step 1 Rub the
insides of each fish
with a teaspoonful
of salt, scrubbing
briskly to remove
any discolored
membranes.

Step 3 Using a
sharp knife, cut 2
diagonal slits on the
side of each fish,
taking great care not
to cut right through
the flesh.

Cook's Notes

	Time		Cook's Tip		Serving Idea
	Preparation takes about 15 minutes, cooking takes 10-16 minutes.		Use herring or mackerel in place of the snapper to vary the menus.		Using 1 small red snapper per person, this recipe could be served as an appetizer.

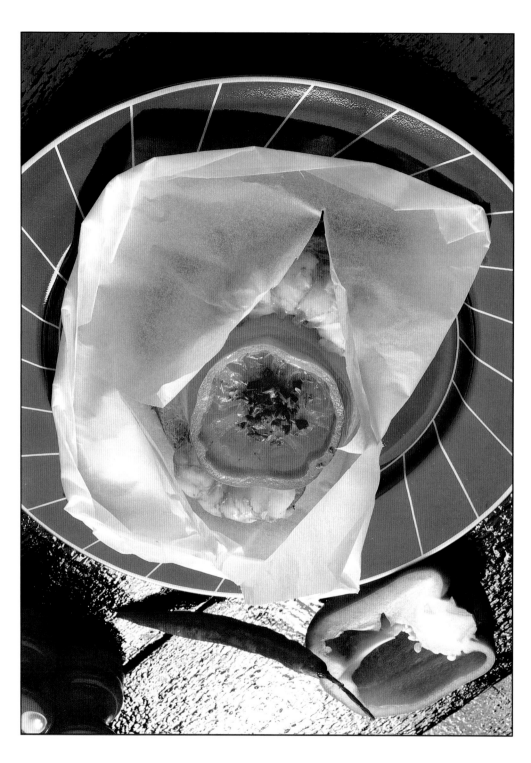

BAKED TUNA PARCELS

This recipe uses a French technique called "en papillote."
Californians, quick to spot a healthy cooking method, use it
often with fish.

Oil
4 tuna steaks, about 8oz each in weight
1 red onion, thinly sliced
1 beefsteak tomato, cut in 4 slices
1 green pepper, seeded and cut in thin rings
8 large, uncooked peeled shrimp
2 tsps finely chopped fresh oregano
Salt
4 tbsps dry white wine or lemon juice

5. Spoon the wine or lemon juice over each fish and fold the wax paper over the fish.

6. Overlap the edges and pinch and fold to seal securely. Place the parcels on a baking sheet.

7. Bake for about 10-12 minutes in a preheated 400°F oven.

8. Unwrap each parcel at the table to serve.

Steps 1-4 Layer the ingredients on oiled wax paper.

Step 6 Overlap the edges of the paper, but don't enclose fish too tightly.

1. Lightly oil 4 oval pieces of wax paper about 8 × 10 inches.

2. Place a tuna steak on half of each piece of paper and top with 2 slices of onion.

3. Place a slice of tomato on each fish and top with green pepper rings.

4. Place 2 shrimp on top and sprinkle over the oregano and salt.

Step 6 Use thumb and forefinger to pinch and fold the overlapped edge to seal.

Cook's Notes

 Time
Preparation takes about 35 minutes and cooking takes about 10-12 minutes.

 Serving Idea
Keep the meal healthy by serving with baked potatoes.

 Cook's Tip
The dish may be prepared up to 6 hours in advance and kept in the refrigerator. Remove about 30 minutes before cooking and allow fish to come to room temperature.

VEAL SCALOPPINE WITH PROSCIUTTO AND CHEESE

Good veal is tender and quick cooking, but expensive. Try this recipe for your next dinner party!

8 veal escalopes
2 tbsps butter or margarine
1 clove garlic, crushed
8 slices prosciutto
3 tbsps sherry
½ cup beef stock (see basic recipes)
1 sprig rosemary
8 slices Mozzarella cheese
Salt and pepper

Step 3 Place a slice of prosciutto on top of each slice of veal and pour over the sherry and stock and add the rosemary.

Step 2 Brown the veal on both sides over medium heat.

Step 6 Place the meat under a preheated broiler and cook to melt the cheese and lightly brown the top.

1. Pound the veal escalopes out thinly between two pieces of wax paper with a meat mallet or a rolling pin.

2. Melt the butter or margarine in a sauté pan over a medium heat and add the veal and garlic. Cook until the veal is lightly browned on both sides.

3. Place a piece of prosciutto on top of each piece of veal and add the sherry, stock and sprig of rosemary to the pan. Cover the pan and cook the veal for about 10 minutes over a low heat, or until done.

4. Remove the meat to a heatproof serving dish and top each piece of veal with a slice of cheese.

5. Bring the cooking liquid to the boil over a high heat and allow to boil rapidly to reduce slightly.

6. Meanwhile, broil the veal under a medium heat to melt and brown the cheese. Remove the sprig of rosemary from the sauce and pour the sauce around the meat to serve.

Cook's Notes

Time
Preparation takes about 15 minutes, cooking takes 15-20 minutes.

Cook's Tip
White wine may be substituted for the sherry, if desired. 1 tsp of tomato paste may be added to the sauce. Use chicken, turkey or pork instead of the veal.

Serving Idea
New potatoes and snow peas would make good accompaniments to this dish.

SERVES 8-10

ALABAMA COLA GLAZED HAM

Don't be afraid to try this somewhat unusual approach to roast
ham. Cola gives it a marvelous taste and color.

10-lb joint country or Smithfield ham
4 cups cola soft drink
Handful whole cloves
1 cup packed dark brown sugar

Step 2 Place the ham rind side down in a roasting pan, pour over the cola and bake.

1. Soak the ham overnight.

2. Preheat oven to 350°F. Place the ham rind side down in a roasting pan. Pour over all but 6 tbsps of the cola and bake, uncovered, 1½ hours or until the internal temperature registers 140°F.

3. Baste the ham every 20 minutes with pan juices using a large spoon or a bulb baster.

4. Remove the ham from the oven and allow it to cool for 10-15 minutes. Remove the rind from the ham with a small, sharp knife and score the fat to a depth of ¼ inch. Stick 1 clove in the center of every other diamond.

5. Mix sugar and the remaining cola together and pour or spread over the ham. Raise the oven temperature to 375°F.

6. Return the ham to the oven and bake for 45 minutes, basting every 15 minutes. Cover loosely with foil if the ham begins to brown too much.

7. Allow to stand 15 minutes before slicing.

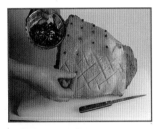

Step 4 Remove the rind from the ham with a small, sharp knife. Stick one clove in the center of every other diamond after scoring the fat.

Step 5 Pour or spread the glaze over the ham before continuing to bake.

Cook's Notes

 Time
Preparation takes about 30 minutes, with overnight soaking for the ham. Cooking takes about 2 hours 15 minutes.

Cook's Tip
Gammon ham requires overnight soaking to remove the saltiness.

Serving Idea
Glazed ham is especially nice served with sweet potatoes and fried okra. Corn bread makes another good accompaniment.

17

SERVES 8

HUNTER'S STEW

A warming and nourishing dish, ideal for those cold winter days.

4 tbsps oil
1 onion
2 cloves garlic, crushed
¾lb stewing steak, pork or venison cut in 2-inch pieces
4 tbsps flour
2 tbsps mild paprika
4 cups light stock
4oz smoked ham, cut in 2-inch pieces
4oz smoked sausage, cut in 2-inch pieces
1 tsp marjoram
1 tsp chopped thyme
1 tsp chopped parsley
Salt and pepper
Pinch cayenne pepper (optional)
2 tbsps tomato paste
1 head white cabbage, chopped
2 apples, cored and chopped
2 carrots, thinly sliced
8 prunes, roughly chopped
3 tomatoes, peeled and roughly chopped
⅓ cup red wine or Madeira
Pinch sugar (optional)

Step 1 To slice an onion, cut in half and then peel. Leave the root end on to hold the onion together and place cut side down on a chopping board.

Step 1 Using a large, sharp knife, slice the onion, keeping the fingers out of the way. Alternatively, hold with a fork.

1. Heat the oil in a large, flameproof casserole over a medium heat. Slice onion thickly and cook with the garlic for 2-3 minutes. Remove and set aside.

2. Add the meat in four small batches, cooking over high heat to brown.

3. When all the meat is browned, return it to the casserole with the onions and garlic. Reduce the heat to medium. Sprinkle over the flour and cook until light brown.

4. Add paprika and cook 1-2 minutes, stirring constantly.

5. Pour on the stock gradually and bring to the boil. Turn down the heat to low and add the smoked meats, herbs, salt, pepper, cayenne and tomato paste.

6. Stir well, cover and cook over low heat for 45 minutes. Stir occasionally and add more liquid if necessary during cooking.

7. When the meat is almost tender, add cabbage, apples, carrots and prunes. Cook a further 20 minutes.

8. Add the tomatoes, wine or Madeira and a pinch of sugar, if desired. Cook a further 10 minutes, adjust the seasoning and serve immediately.

Cook's Notes

Time
Preparation takes about 25 minutes and cooking takes about 1 hour 25 minutes in total.

Cook's Tip
Use a combination of beef, pork and venison for a tasty variation.

Serving Idea
Accompany with rice, mashed potatoes or bread. The stew may be eaten hot or cold.

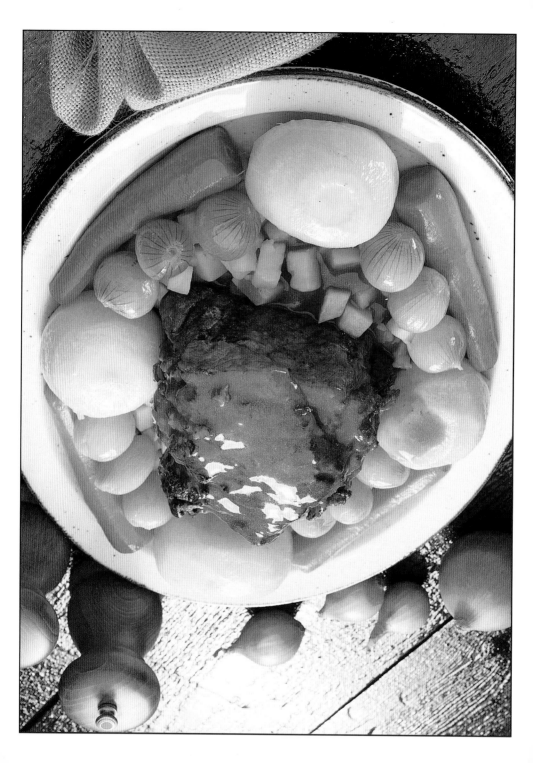

YANKEE POT ROAST

This classic American recipe has its roots in French and German cuisine. It is an excellent way of cooking economical cuts of beef.

3-lb beef roast (rump, chuck, round or top end)
Flour seasoned with salt and pepper
4 tbsps butter or margarine
1 onion stuck with 2 cloves
1 bay leaf
2 tsps fresh thyme or 1 tsp dried thyme
1 cup beef stock (see basic recipes)
4 carrots
12 small onions, peeled
4 small turnips, peeled and left whole
2 potatoes, cut into even-sized pieces
2 tbsps all-purpose flour

1. Dredge the beef with the seasoned flour, patting off the excess.

2. Melt half the butter in a large, heavy-based casserole or pan over a medium heat and, when foaming, brown the meat on all sides, turning it with wooden spoons or a spatula.

3. When well browned, add the onion stuck with the cloves, bay leaf and thyme and pour on the stock. Cover the pan, reduce the heat to low and cook on top of the stove or in a preheated 300°F oven. Cook slowly for about 2 hours, adding more liquid, either stock or water, as necessary.

4. Test the meat and, if beginning to feel tender, add the vegetables. Cover and continue to cook until the meat is completely tender and the vegetables are cooked through.

5. Remove the meat and vegetables from the casserole or pan and place them on a warm serving platter. Skim the excess fat from the top of the sauce and bring it back to the boil.

6. Mix the remaining butter and the all-purpose flour to a smooth paste. Add about 1 tsp of the mixture to the boiling sauce and beat thoroughly with a whisk. Continue adding the mixture until the sauce is of the desired thickness. Carve the meat and spoon over some of the sauce. Serve the rest of the sauce separately.

Step 2 Place the meat in the hot butter to brown. Use wooden spoons or a spatula to turn.

Step 6 To thicken the sauce at the end, add a small spoonful of flour and butter paste and beat well.

Cook's Notes

Time
Preparation takes about 30 minutes and cooking takes about 2-2½ hours.

Cook's Tip
The flour and butter paste, or beurre manié, may be prepared in large quantities and kept in the refrigerator or freezer to use any time thickening is necessary for a sauce.

Serving Idea
This dish can be a meal in itself. If an accompaniment is desired, serve a green vegetable or a salad.

SOUTHWESTERN STIR-FRY

East meets West in a dish that is lightning-fast to cook.

1lb sirloin or rump steak
2 cloves garlic, crushed
6 tbsps wine vinegar
6 tbsps oil
Pinch sugar, salt and pepper
1 bay leaf
1 tbsp ground cumin
Oil
1 small sweet red pepper, seeded and sliced
1 small green pepper, seeded and sliced
2oz baby corn
4 green onions, shredded

Red Sauce
4 tbsps oil
1 medium onion, finely chopped
1-2 hot green chili peppers, finely chopped
1-2 cloves garlic, crushed
8 fresh ripe tomatoes, peeled, seeded and chopped
6 sprigs fresh coriander
3 tbsps tomato paste

Step 1 Slice the meat thinly across the grain.

1. Slice the meat thinly across the grain. Combine in a plastic bag with the next 6 ingredients. Tie the bag and toss the ingredients inside to coat. Place in a bowl and leave about 4 hours.

2. Heat the oil for the sauce over a medium heat and cook the onion, chili peppers and garlic to soften but not brown. Add remaining sauce ingredients and cook about 15 minutes over a low heat. Purée in a food processor until smooth.

3. Heat oil in a skillet over a medium heat and add the meat in three batches, discarding the marinade. Cook to brown and set aside. Add about 2 tbsps of oil and cook the peppers about 2 minutes. Add the corn and onions and return the meat to the pan. Cook another minute and add the sauce. Cook to heat through and serve immediately.

Step 3 Cook the meat quickly over high heat to brown.

Step 3 Add the remaining ingredients and enough sauce to coat all ingredients thoroughly.

Cook's Notes

Time
Preparation takes about 25 minutes, plus 4 hours for marinating the meat. The sauce takes about 15 minutes to cook and the remaining ingredients need about 6-7 minutes.

 Cook's Tip
The sauce may be prepared ahead of time and kept in the refrigerator for several days. It may also be frozen. Defrost the sauce at room temperature and then boil rapidly to reduce it again slightly.

 Serving Idea
Serve with rice or warm tortillas and a salad.

BARBECUED RIBS

Popular with all the family, barbecued ribs are surprisingly easy to prepare with a sweet, spicy flavor. The versatile sauce keeps well in the refrigerator, too.

4½lbs pork spare ribs

Sauce
1 cup tomato ketchup
2 tsps mustard powder
4 tbsps Worcestershire sauce
2 tbsps vinegar
4 tbsps brown sugar
Half a green chili pepper, seeded and finely chopped
Half a small onion, finely chopped
4 tbsps water
Salt (if necessary)

Step 3 Uncover the ribs and pour over the sauce.

Step 4 To serve, cut the ribs into individual pieces between the bones.

Step 1 Cook the ribs in a roasting pan at a high temperature for 15 minutes.

1. Place the ribs in a roasting pan and cover with foil. Cook for 15 minutes at 425°F.

2. Meanwhile, combine all the sauce ingredients in a heavy-based pan and bring to the boil over a medium heat. Reduce heat to low and simmer for about 15 minutes.

3. Reduce the oven temperature to 350°F and uncover the ribs. Pour over the sauce and bake a further hour, basting frequently.

4. Remove the ribs from the roasting pan and reserve the sauce. Place the ribs on a cutting board and slice into individual rib pieces, between the bones.

5. Skim any fat from the surface of the sauce, add salt if necessary and serve the sauce separately.

Cook's Notes

Time
Preparation takes about 30 minutes and cooking takes about 1 hour 15 minutes.

Cook's Tip
The sauce is also good served on pork chops, chicken or steaks.

Serving Idea
Serve with boiled rice and a green salad. Add warm tortillas to complement the dish.

COUNTRY HAM WITH BOURBON RAISIN SAUCE

The tart and sweet flavor of this sauce has long been the
choice to complement savory country ham.

8 ¼-inch slices country or Smithfield ham
Milk
Oil or margarine

Sauce
1½ tbsps cornstarch
1 cup apple cider
½ tsp ginger or allspice
2 tsps lemon juice
2 tbsps bourbon
2oz raisins
Pinch salt

Step 1 Before browning the ham, snip the edges at intervals of ½ inch with kitchen scissors. This will prevent the ham slices from curling.

1. Soak the ham slices in enough milk to barely cover for at
least 30 minutes. Rinse and pat dry. Trim off the rind and
discard it, and snip the edges at ½-inch intervals to prevent
curling.

2. Heat a small amount of oil or margarine in a large skillet
over a medium-high heat and brown the ham slices about
2 minutes per side.

3. Mix the cornstarch with about 6 tbsps of the apple cider
and deglaze the skillet with the remaining cider. Stir in the
ginger or allspice and the lemon juice.

4. Stirring constantly, pour in the cornstarch mixture and
bring the liquid to the boil. Cook and stir constantly until
thickened. Add the bourbon and raisins and cook a further
5 minutes. Add salt to taste. Reheat the ham quickly, if
necessary, and pour over the sauce to serve.

Step 4 Stirring constantly, pour in the cornstarch mixture.

Step 4 When the raisins are added to the sauce, cook a further five mintues, or until the raisins are plumped and softened.

Cook's Notes

Time
Preparation takes about 20 minutes, with at least 30 minutes' soaking in milk for the ham. Cooking takes about 2 minutes per side for the ham and about 10 minutes for the sauce.

Cook's Tip
Soaking country or Smithfield ham in milk will help to remove the saltiness, giving it an improved, milder flavor.

Serving Idea
For a delicious family supper, accompany with baked potatoes and a green vegetable.

PEPPERED STEAK

A classic way of serving steak, peppered steaks are simple to
prepare and wonderful to eat.

4 rump or fillet steaks
Oil
2 tbsps black peppercorns, lightly crushed
4 tbsps butter
Salt
4 tbsps brandy
3 tbsps light cream
Watercress, to garnish

1. Brush the steaks on both sides with the oil, then coat
with the black peppercorns. Crush these into the steak
with a steak hammer.

2. Over a high heat, melt the butter in a skillet and cook the
steaks for about 1½ minutes on each side.

3. Reduce the heat and cook for a further 2 minutes for a
rare steak, 3 minutes for a medium steak, or 7 minutes for a
well-done steak. Season with salt.

4. Warm the brandy in a ladle near the heat. Taking great
care, set the brandy alight and pour it over the steaks.

5. Remove the steaks and place on a warmed serving
dish. Keep warm.

6. Stir the cream into the juices in the skillet and heat over
a low heat for a few minutes.

Step 1 Coat the
steaks with the
lightly crushed black
peppercorns and
crush these into the
meat with a steak
hammer.

Step 4 Very
carefully, ignite the
warm brandy in a
ladle and pour it
over the steaks.

7. Pour the sauce over the steaks and garnish with the
watercress.

Cook's Notes

 Time
Preparation takes about
15 minutes, and cooking
takes between 5 and 15 minutes,
depending on whether a rare,
medium or well-done steak is
required.

 Cook's Tip
If you prefer, the steaks can
be broiled, instead of pan-
cooked. The cooking times should be
about the same, and the sauce can
be prepared separately.

 Serving Idea
Serve with new potatoes, or
French fries, and a large,
fresh salad.

SOUTH SEAS MEATBALLS

An unusual way of serving a favorite family meal.

1lb extra lean ground beef
1 egg, beaten
Salt and pepper
1 tbsp sunflower oil
3 small shallots, chopped
2 tbsps whole-wheat flour
1lb canned pineapple chunks in natural juice
1 tbsp soy sauce
1 tsp wine vinegar
½ green pepper, seeded and finely chopped
¼ cup blanched slivered almonds

1. Put the beef into a large bowl and mix in the egg and the seasoning.

2. Divide the beef mixture into 8, and roll into balls. Dust your hands lightly with flour, and flatten each ball slightly.

3. Brush the meat balls with a little of the oil, and broil under a hot broiler for 10-15 minutes, turning them once during cooking, to cook each side.

4. Heat the remaining oil in a skillet over a low heat and cook the shallots gently for 3 minutes, until they are transparent, but not brown.

5. Stir the flour into the shallots, and cook for about 1 minute.

6. Add the juices from the canned pineapple gradually to the flour mixture, stirring well between additions, until all the juice is incorporated and the sauce is smooth.

Step 2 Divide the beef mixture into 8, and shape into 8 balls. Flatten the balls slightly with lightly floured hands.

Step 3 Brush the meatballs with a little oil, and arrange them on a lined broiler pan, before broiling.

7. Add the soy sauce and vinegar, and season with salt and pepper.

8. Stir the pineapple chunks, green pepper and almonds into the sauce.

9. Add the cooked meatballs to the sauce and heat gently for about 10-15 minutes until they are warmed right through.

Cook's Notes

Time
Preparation takes about 20 minutes, and cooking will take about 40 minutes.

Cook's Tip
Use 1lb ground chicken for an interesting variation.

Serving Idea
Serve the meatballs in the sauce, surrounded by a bed of rice.

ROAST HERBED LEG OF LAMB

The next time you cook a leg of lamb for the Sunday roast, try
this recipe for an interesting and delicious change.

3½-lb leg of lamb
2-3 cloves garlic
2 bay leaves
½ cup margarine
1½ cups bread crumbs
1 tsp chopped fresh thyme
1 tsp chopped fresh rosemary
1 tbsp chopped fresh parsley
Juice 2 lemons
Salt and pepper

Step 3 Spread the margarine, bread crumb and herb mixture over the upper surface of the meat using a round-bladed knife.

Step 2 Make small slits in the underside of the leg of lamb, and insert thin slices of garlic into these.

Step 5 Half an hour before the end of the cooking time, roll back the foil and baste the joint with the meat juices.

1. Prepare a sheet of foil large enough to wrap around the meat completely.

2. Peel and slice 1 or 2 of the garlic cloves. Make small cuts in the underside of the meat and insert the slices of garlic into these. Put the meat onto the foil with the bay leaves underneath.

3. In a small bowl, mix the margarine thoroughly with the remaining ingredients, crushing the last garlic clove before

adding it. Spread this mixture over the upper surface of the meat, using a wetted round-bladed knife.

4. Loosely wrap the foil around the joint of meat, place in a roasting pan and roast in a preheated oven, 400°F, for about 1¾ hours.

5. Unwrap the foil and baste the meat with the melted fat that has collected in the base of the pan.

6. Continue roasting, uncovered, for a further 30 minutes, until the crust is brown and crisp.

Cook's Notes

 Time
Preparation takes about 15 minutes, and cooking takes about 30 minutes per 1lb, plus 30 minutes. This may be reduced to 25 minutes per 1lb, plus 25 minutes extra cooking, if you like slightly rarer meat.

Cook's Tip
The bread crumb mixture in this recipe is also delicious when used to coat a joint of gammon.

 Serving Idea
Serve with turned vegetables (see garnish section) for a very stylish meal.

VEAL WITH SORREL AND CHEESE STUFFING

Sorrel gives this dish a unique flavor. If sorrel is unavailable,
use fresh spinach instead.

2-lb rolled roast of veal
½ cup garlic cheese spread
4oz sorrel leaf, finely chopped
2½ tsps fresh oregano or marjoram, chopped
½ cup finely chopped walnuts
Freshly ground black pepper
½ cup all-purpose flour
⅔ tsp paprika
1 egg, beaten
1 cup dried bread crumbs
3¾ tbsps unsalted butter, melted

Step 2 Spread the filling ingredients evenly over the inside of the meat.

1. Unroll the veal roast and trim off some of the fat from the outside using a sharp knife.

2. Put the cheese, sorrel, oregano or marjoram, walnuts and black pepper into a bowl. Mix together using a round-bladed knife or your hands, until the ingredients are well bound together. Spread this filling over the inside of the veal.

3. Roll the veal roast up, jelly-roll fashion, and sew the ends together with a trussing needle and thick thread.

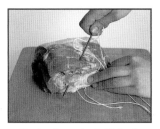

Step 3 Sew the ends of the joint together using a trussing needle and strong thread.

.. Dredge the veal roll with the flour and sprinkle with the paprika. Press this coating well onto the meat using your hands.

5. Brush the floured meat liberally with beaten egg and roll it into the dried bread crumbs, pressing gently to make sure that all surfaces are thoroughly coated.

6. Place the coated veal on a cookie sheet, brush with melted butter and roast in a preheated oven 325°F, for 1 hour, or until the meat is well cooked.

7. Allow to stand for 10 minutes before slicing and serving hot, or allow to cool, then chill and serve cold.

Cook's Notes

Time
Preparation takes 25 minutes, cooking takes 1-1½ hours.

Cook's Tip
This recipe will freeze well, and is ideal prepared in advance and served cold, after being thawed.

Serving Idea
Serve with salad or vegetables and a rich brown sauce.

SPICED PORK

Five spice is a ready-prepared spicy powder which can easily
be obtained from delicatessens or ethnic supermarkets. It is
used in this dish with ginger and pepper to make a typical
Szechuan meal.

Ilb pork fillet
5 tbsps sesame oil
1-inch piece fresh ginger, peeled and chopped
1¼ tsps black peppercorns
1¼ tsps five spice powder
¼ cup dry sherry
⅔ cup light stock
3 tbsps honey
4 green onions, cut into diagonal slices
⅓ cup bamboo shoots, shredded
1 large ripe mango, peeled and sliced

1. Using a sharp knife, finely slice the pork fillet into thin
strips.

2. Put the oil into a wok or large skillet, and heat gently
over a low heat. Add the ginger and stir this into the oil.
Cook quickly for 20-30 seconds.

3. Add the sliced meat to the wok and stir-fry for 4-5 minutes, or until the meat is well cooked and tender.

Step 3 Stir-fry the meat with the oil and ginger.

Step 5 Add the onions, bamboo shoots and mango to the cooked pork, stirring continuously to cook evenly.

Step 1 Using a sharp knife, slice the pork into thin strips.

4. Stir the peppercorns, five spice powder, sherry, stock
and honey into the meat. Mix well and bring to the boil over
a high heat.

5. Add all the remaining ingredients to the wok and cook
quickly, stirring all the time for a further 3 minutes.

6. Serve immediately.

Cook's Notes

Time
Preparation takes
25 minutes, cooking takes
about 10 minutes.

Cook's Tip
Use chicken instead of
pork in this recipe to ring
the changes.

Serving Idea
Serve with rice or Chinese
noodles.

PEPPERED FILLET OF LAMB WITH FRUIT

An unusual yet delicious combination of meat and fruit.

8oz dried fruit salad
2¼lbs lamb neck fillets
1 tbsp coarsely crushed black peppercorns
4 tbsps butter or margarine
2 tbsps flour
1 cup light stock
½ cup medium dry sherry
3 tbsps heavy cream
Pinch salt
Watercress to garnish

Step 3 Cook the lamb fillet in a sauté pan or skillet to brown evenly on all sides.

Step 2 Press the peppercorns firmly into the surface of each lamb fillet using your hand, a meat mallet or rolling pin.

5. Drain the fruit, add to the pan and return the lamb fillet. Cover and cook over a low heat for about 15-20 minutes until lamb and fruit are tender.

6. When the lamb is cooked, remove it from the pan and slice into diagonal pieces about ¼ inch thick. Arrange on serving plate and add the cooked fruit.

7. Add the cream and salt to the sauce and bring to the boil. Allow to boil 1 minute to thicken and cook the cream and spoon the sauce over the fruit and meat to serve. Garnish with watercress.

1. Place the fruit salad in a saucepan, cover with water and bring to the boil over a high heat. Once the water boils, remove from the heat and leave to soak for about 2 hours.

2. Sprinkle the black peppercorns on the lamb fillets and press them in firmly with the palm of your hand, or bat them lightly with a meat mallet or rolling pin.

3. Melt the butter or margarine in a large sauté pan over a medium-high heat and when foaming, add the lamb fillets. Cook to seal on both sides. When the lamb fillets are brown, remove them to a plate and set them aside.

4. Add the flour to the pan and cook over a medium heat to brown slightly. Stir in the stock gradually to blend well and add the sherry. Bring to the boil.

Step 6 When lamb is cooked, slice it thinly on the diagonal.

Cook's Notes

Time
Preparation takes about 25 minutes, with 2 hours, soaking time for the fruit. Cooking takes about 30-40 minutes.

Cook's Tip
When coating the fillets with peppercorns, press firmly so that they stick well in the surface and do not fall off during cooking.

Serving Idea
This sumptuous dish makes an ideal main course for a dinner party or special family occasion.

MEXICAN BEEF PATTIES

Refried beans added to the meat mixture make moist and
flavorsome beefburgers that are slightly out of the ordinary.

1 onion, finely chopped
1 tbsp oil
12oz ground beef
8oz canned refried beans
4 tbsps bread crumbs
½ tsp cumin
1 tsp chili powder
1 clove garlic, crushed
Salt and pepper
1 egg, beaten
Flour to coat
Oil
Watercress to garnish

1. Cook the onion in the oil over a medium heat until soft
but not browned. Remove from the heat and mix in the
beef, beans, bread crumbs, spices, garlic and seasoning
and gradually add the egg until the mixture holds together
well.

2. Turn the mixture out onto a well-floured surface and
divide into 8 pieces.

3. Shape into even-sized patties with well-floured hands.
Knead the pieces before shaping, if necessary, to make
sure mixture holds together with no cracks.

4. Coat lightly with flour and refrigerate until firm.

5. Pour enough oil into a large skillet to completely cover
the patties and heat over a medium heat until hot. Cook 2 at
a time until golden brown on all sides and completely
cooked through.

6. Remove from the skillet and drain on paper towels.
Arrange on a serving plate and garnish with watercress.

Step 3 Shape meat mixture into firm, even-sized patties with well-floured hands.

Step 4 Coat lightly with flour on all sides and place on a plate or baking sheet to refrigerate until firm.

Step 5 Cook 2 patties at a time in hot oil. Make sure they are completely submerged.

Cook's Notes

Time
Preparation takes about 20 minutes. The patties will take at least 1 hour to firm up sufficiently in the refrigerator.

Cook's Tip
If mixture is too soft to shape, add 2 tbsps flour.

Serving Idea
Serve with sour cream or taco sauce and an avocado and tomato salad. Accompany with warm flour tortillas.

SOUTHERN FRIED CHICKEN

No discussion of Southern cooking is complete without
mentioning fried chicken. Eating it is even better than talking
about it!

3lbs frying chicken portions
2 eggs
2 cups flour
1 tsp each salt, paprika and sage
½ tsp black pepper
Pinch cayenne pepper (optional)
Oil
Parsley or watercress

1. Rinse chicken and pat dry.

2. Beat the eggs in a large bowl and add the chicken one piece at a time, turning to coat.

3. Mix flour and seasonings in a large paper or plastic bag.

4. Place chicken pieces coated with egg into the bag one at a time, close bag tightly and shake to coat each piece of chicken. Alternatively, dip each coated chicken piece in a

Step 2 Dip the chicken pieces in the egg to coat them well.

Step 4 Coat the chicken on all sides with flour, shaking off the excess.

Step 6 Cook the chicken skin side down first for 12 minutes, turn over and fry a further 12 minutes.

bowl of seasoned flour, shaking off the excess.

5. Heat oil in a large skillet or wok to the depth of about ½ inch.

6. When the oil is hot, add the chicken skin side down first. Cook about 12 minutes and then turn over. Cook a further 12 minutes or until the juices run clear.

7. Drain the chicken on paper towels and serve immediately. Garnish serving plate with parsley or watercress.

Cook's Notes

Time
Preparation takes about 20 minutes and cooking takes about 24 minutes.

Cook's Tip
When coating anything for frying, be sure to coat it just before cooking. If left to stand, coating will usually become very soggy.

Serving Idea
Serve with a variety of relishes to complement the dish.

SERVES 4

PECAN CHICKEN

Pecans are often used in the South in both sweet and savory dishes. Here, their rich, sweet taste complements a stuffing for chicken.

4 boned chicken breasts
3 tbsps butter or margarine
1 small onion, finely chopped
3oz pork sausage meat
3oz fresh bread crumbs
1 tsp chopped thyme
1 tsp chopped parsley
Salt and pepper
1 small egg, lightly beaten
1 cup pecan halves
1 cup chicken stock
1 tbsp flour
2 tbsps sherry
1 bunch watercress to garnish

1. Cut a small pocket in the side of each chicken breast using a small knife.

2. Melt 1 tbsp butter in a small saucepan and add the onion. Cook a few minutes over a low heat to soften. Add the sausage meat and turn up the heat to brown. Break up the sausage meat with a fork as it cooks.

Step 1 Use a small, sharp knife to cut a pocket in each chicken breast.

Step 4 Open each pocket in the chicken and spoon in the stuffing.

3. Drain any excess fat and add the bread crumbs, herbs and a pinch of salt and pepper. Allow to cool slightly and add enough egg to hold the mixture together. Chop pecans, reserving 8, and add to the stuffing.

4. Using a small teaspoon, fill the pocket in each chicken breast with some of the stuffing.

5. Melt 1 tbsp butter in a casserole and place in the chicken breasts, skin side down first. Brown over a medium heat and turn over. Brown the other side quickly to seal.

6. Pour in the stock, cover the casserole and cook for about 25-30 minutes in a preheated 350°F oven until tender.

7. When chicken is cooked, remove it to a serving plate to keep warm. Reserve cooking liquid.

8. Melt remaining butter in a small saucepan over a medium heat and stir in the flour. Cook to a pale straw color. Strain on the cooking liquid and add the sherry. Bring to the boil and stir constantly until thickened. Add the pecans and seasoning.

9. Spoon some of the sauce over the chicken. Garnish with watercress and the reserved whole pecans.

Cook's Notes

Time
Preparation takes about 30 minutes and cooking takes about 40 minutes.

Cook's Tip
If pecans are unavailable use hazelnuts. Crush the hazelnuts roughly for the garnish and brown lightly in the butter before adding flour for the sauce.

Serving Idea
Serve with a combination of white and wild rice.

CHICKEN CACCIATORE

The use of herbs, wine and vinegar in this delicious Italian
family meal gives a wonderful, hearty flavor without the need
for salt.

5 tbsps olive oil
3lb chicken pieces
2 onions, sliced
3 cloves garlic, minced
8oz button mushrooms, quartered
½ cup red wine
1¼ tbsps wine vinegar
1¼ tbsps fresh chopped parsley
2½ tsps fresh chopped oregano
2½ tsps fresh chopped basil
1 bay leaf
1lb canned tomatoes
½ cup chicken stock
Freshly ground black pepper
Pinch of sugar

1. In a large skillet heat the oil over a medium heat and lay the chicken pieces, skin side down, in one layer.

2. Brown for 3-4 minutes, then turn each piece over. Con-tinue turning the chicken portions until all surfaces are well browned.

3. Remove the chicken portions to a plate and keep warm.

4. Add the onions and garlic to the oil and chicken juices in the skillet. Cook lightly for 2-3 minutes, or until they are just beginning to brown.

5. Add the mushrooms to the skillet and cook for about 1 minute, stirring constantly.

6. Pour the wine and vinegar into the pan and boil rapidly over a high heat to reduce to about half the original quantity.

7. Add the herbs, bay leaf and tomatoes, stirring well to break up the tomatoes.

8. Stir in the chicken stock and season with pepper and sugar.

9. Return the chicken to the tomato sauce and cover with a tight-fitting lid. Reduce the heat, simmer for about 1 hour, or until the chicken is tender.

Step 2 Turn the chicken frequently until all the outer surfaces are golden brown.

Step 7 Break up the tomatoes in the skillet by pressing them gently with the back of a wooden spoon.

Cook's Notes

 Time
Preparation takes about 20 minutes, cooking takes 1 hour 15 minutes.

 Cook's Tip
This dish freezes well for up to 3 months. Defrost thoroughly and reheat by simmering for at least 30 minutes before serving.

Serving Idea
Serve with rice or pasta, and a mixed salad.

CHICKEN LIVER STIR-FRY

Chicken livers are very low in fat and high in flavor. They also
require very little cooking so are perfect for stir-fry recipes.

1lb chicken livers, trimmed
4½ tbsps sesame oil
⅓ cup split blanched almonds
1 clove garlic, peeled
⅓ cup snow peas, trimmed
8-10 Chinese cabbage leaves, shredded
3 tsps cornstarch
1½ tbsps cold water
3 tbsps soy sauce
⅔ cup chicken or vegetable stock

1. Cut the chicken livers into even-sized pieces.

Step 1 Cut the chicken livers into even-sized pieces.

2. Heat a wok over a medium heat and pour in the oil. When the oil is hot, reduce the heat to low and stir-fry the almonds until they are pale golden brown. Remove the almonds, draining any oil back into the wok, and set them aside on paper towels.

3. Add the garlic clove to the wok and cook for 1-2 minutes to flavor the oil only. Remove the clove of garlic and discard.

4. Stir the chicken livers into the flavored oil and cook for 2-3 minutes, stirring frequently to brown evenly. Remove

Step 2 Stir-fry the almonds in the hot oil until they are a pale golden brown.

the chicken livers from the wok and set them aside.

5. Add the snow peas to the hot oil and stir-fry for 1 minute. Then stir in the Chinese cabbage leaves and cook for 1 minute further. Remove the vegetables and set aside.

6. Mix together the cornstarch and water, then blend in the soy sauce and stock.

7. Pour the cornstarch mixture into the wok and bring to the boil, stirring until the sauce has thickened and cleared.

8. Return all other ingredients to the wok and heat through for 1 minute. Serve immediately.

Step 7 Cook the sauce in the wok, stirring all the time until it has thickened and cleared.

Cook's Notes

Time
Preparation takes 25 minutes, cooking takes 5-6 minutes.

Cook's Tip
Use finely sliced lamb's or calfs' liver in place of the chicken livers as a delicious alternative.

Serving Idea
Serve with fried rice or noodles.

CHICKEN MOGHLAI WITH CORIANDER CHUTNEY

The creamy spiciness of the chicken is a good contrast to the hotness of the chutney.

4 tbsps oil
3lbs chicken pieces, skinned
1 tsp ground cardamon
½ tsp ground cinnamon
1 bay leaf
4 cloves
2 onions, finely chopped
1-inch piece fresh ginger, grated
4 cloves garlic, crushed
¼ cup ground almonds
2 tsps cumin seeds
Pinch cayenne pepper
1 cup light cream
6 tbsps plain yogurt
2 tbsps roasted cashew nuts
2 tbsps golden raisins
Salt

Chutney
3oz fresh coriander leaves
1 green chili pepper, chopped and seeded
1 tbsp lemon juice
Salt and pepper
Pinch sugar
1 tbsp oil
½ tsp ground coriander

1. To prepare the chicken, heat the oil in a large skillet over a medium heat. Cook the chicken pieces on each side until golden brown.

2. Remove the chicken and set aside. Put the cardamom, cinnamon, bay leaf and cloves into the hot oil and meat

Step 7 Stir the yogurt, cashews and golden raisins into the chicken. Heat through gently to plump up the golden raisins, but do not allow the mixture to boil.

juices and cook for 30 seconds. Stir in the onions and cook until soft but not brown.

3. Stir the ginger, garlic, almonds, cumin and cayenne pepper into the onions. Reduce the heat to low and cook gently for 2-3 minutes, then stir in the cream.

4. Return the chicken pieces to the skillet, along with any juices. Cover and simmer for 30-40 minutes, or until the chicken is cooked and tender.

5. While the chicken is cooking, prepare the chutney. Put the coriander leaves, chili pepper, lemon, seasoning and sugar into a blender or food processor and work to a paste.

6. Heat the oil over a medium heat and cook the ground coriander for 1 minute. Add this mixture to the processed coriander leaves and blend in thoroughly.

7. Just before serving, stir the yogurt, cashews and golden raisins into the chicken. Heat through over a low heat just enough to plump up the golden raisins, but do not allow the mixture to boil.

8. Serve at once with the coriander chutney.

Cook's Notes

Time
Preparation takes about 25 minutes, and cooking takes about 50 minutes.

Cook's Tip
The coriander chutney can be prepared using a pestle and mortar, if a blender or food processor is not available.

Serving Idea
Serve with boiled rice and a cucumber and tomato salad.

CHICKEN WITH WALNUTS & CELERY

Oyster sauce lends a subtle, slightly salty taste to this
Cantonese dish.

8oz boned chicken, cut into 1-inch pieces
2 tsps soy sauce
2 tsps brandy
1 tsp cornstarch
Salt and pepper
2 tbsps oil
1 clove garlic
1 cup walnut halves
3 celery stalks
2 tsps oyster sauce
½ cup water or chicken stock

1. Combine the chicken with the soy sauce, brandy, cornstarch, salt and pepper.

2. Heat a wok over a medium heat and add the oil and garlic. Cook for about 1 minute to flavor the oil.

3. Remove the garlic and add the chicken in two batches.

Step 3 Cook the chicken until done but not brown.

Step 3 Add the walnuts to the wok and cook until they are crisp.

Step 4 Use a large, sharp knife to cut the celery on the diagonal into thin slices.

Stir-fry quickly without allowing the chicken to brown. Remove the chicken and add the walnuts to the wok. Cook for about 2 minutes until the walnuts are slightly brown and crisp.

4. Slice the celery, add to the wok and cook for about 1 minute. Add the oyster sauce and water and bring to the boil. When boiling, return the chicken to the pan and stir to coat all the ingredients well. Serve immediately.

Cook's Notes

 Time
Preparation takes about 20 minutes, cooking takes about 8 minutes.

Cook's Tip
Nuts can burn very easily. Stir them constantly for even browning.

 Serving Idea
Serve with boiled or fried rice.

CORNISH GAME HEN WITH SPICY SAUCE

Although this recipe takes quite a while to prepare, the end result will make your effort worthwhile.

4 Cornish game hens
1¼ tsps each of paprika, mustard powder and ground ginger
¾ tsp ground turmeric
Pinch ground allspice
5 tbsps unsalted butter
2½ tbsps chili sauce
1¼ tbsps plum chutney
1¼ tbsps brown sauce
1¼ tbsps Worcestershire sauce
1¼ tbsps soy sauce
Dash Tabasco sauce
4 tbsps chicken stock

1. Tie the legs of each hen together and tuck them under the wing tips.

2. Put the paprika, mustard, ginger, turmeric and allspice, into a small bowl and mix together well.

3. Rub the spice mixture evenly on all sides of the four birds, taking great care to push some behind the wings and into the joints.

4. Refrigerate the game hens for at least 1 hour.

5. Arrange the hens in a roasting pan. Melt the butter and brush it evenly over the birds. Roast in a preheated oven, 350°F, for 20 minutes, brushing with the roasting juices during this time.

6. Put the chili sauce, plum chutney, brown sauce, Worcestershire sauce, soy sauce and Tabasco and chicken stock into a small bowl and mix well.

7. Brush about half of this sauce over the birds. Return to the oven and cook for a further 40 minutes.

8. Brush the hens twice more with the remaining sauce mixture during this final cooking time so that the skins become brown and crisp.

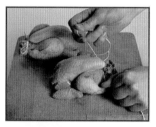

Step 1 Tie the legs of each bird together with trussing thread and tuck them under the wing tips.

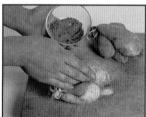

Step 3 Rub the hens all over with the spice mixture, pressing it down into the wings and joints.

Cook's Notes

Time
Preparation takes about 25 minutes, plus 1 hour standing time. Cooking takes 60-70 minutes, depending on the size of the birds.

Cook's Tip
This dish freezes well for up to 3 months.

Serving Idea
Serve with fresh cooked pasta and a large salad.

SERVES 4

TURKEY MARSALA

Marsala is a dessert wine from Sicily which complements
chicken, veal or turkey surprisingly well. It is traditional, but
sherry will serve as a substitute if Marsala is unavailable.

4 turkey breast fillets or escalopes
4 tbsps butter or margarine
1 clove garlic
4 anchovy fillets, soaked in milk
4 slices Mozzarella cheese
Capers
2 tsps chopped marjoram
1 tbsp chopped parsley
3 tbsps Marsala
½ cup heavy cream
Salt and pepper

1. Flatten the turkey breasts between two sheets of wax
paper with a meat mallet or rolling pin if necessary.

2. Melt butter in a sauté pan over a medium heat and,
when foaming, add the garlic and the turkey. Cook for a few
minutes on each side until lightly browned. Remove the
fillets from the pan.

3. Drain the anchovy fillets and rinse them well. Dry on
paper towels. Put a slice of cheese on top of each turkey
fillet and arrange the anchovies and capers on top of each.
Sprinkle with the chopped herbs and return the turkey to
the pan.

4. Cook the turkey a further 5 minutes over a medium heat,
until the turkey is done and the cheese has melted. Remove to a serving dish and keep warm. Return the pan to
the heat and add the Marsala. Scrape the browned pan
juices off the bottom and reduce the heat to low. Add the
cream and beat in well with a whisk. Lower the heat and
simmer gently, uncovered, for a few minutes to thicken the
sauce. Season the sauce with salt and pepper and spoon
over the turkey fillets to serve.

Step 1 Flatten the turkey breasts between two sheets of wax paper with a rolling pin or meat mallet.

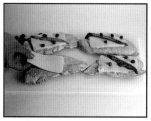

Step 3 Place a slice of cheese on top of each turkey breast and top with anchovies, capers and herbs.

Step 4 Cook until turkey is done and the cheese has melted.

Cook's Notes

 Time
Preparation takes about
25 minutes and cooking
about 20 minutes.

Cook's Tip
Turkey breast fillets are very
lean so can dry out easily if
over-cooked.

 Serving Idea
Accompany the Turkey
Marsala with new potatoes
and lightly cooked zucchini.

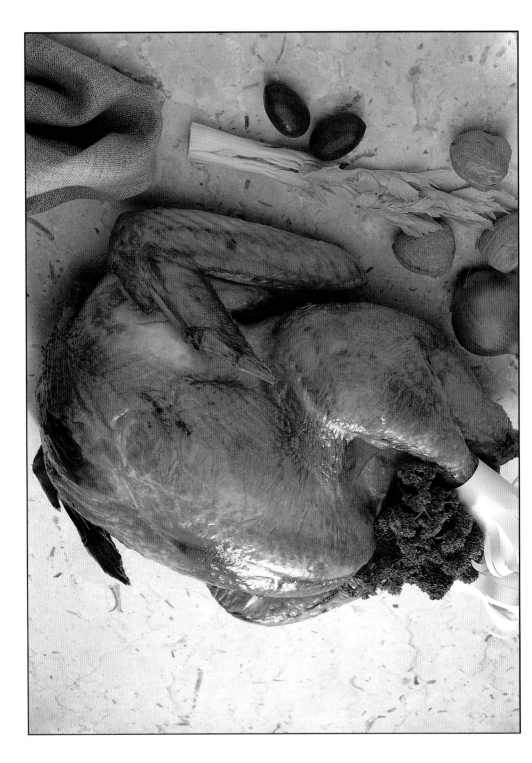

NEW ENGLAND ROAST TURKEY

The Thanksgiving celebration would not be the same without
a turkey on the table. Native Americans first domesticated the
bird and introduced the early settlers to it.

20 lb fresh turkey
⅓ cup butter

Sausage Stuffing
4 tbsps oil
4oz sausage meat
3 celery stalks, diced
2 onions, diced
1 cup chopped walnuts or pecans
1 cup raisins
2 tbsps chopped fresh parsley
1lb day-old bread, made into small cubes
1 cup chicken stock
¼ tsp each dried thyme and sage
Salt and pepper

1. Rinse turkey, removing neck, heart and gizzards. Drain and pat dry.

2. Remove the fat which is just inside the cavity of the bird.

3. To prepare the stuffing, heat the oil over a medium heat and cook the sausage meat breaking it up with a fork as it cooks. Add the celery, onion, nuts and raisins and cook for about 5 minutes, stirring constantly.

4. Drain away the fat and add the herbs, cubes of bread and stock, and mix well. Season to taste.

5. Stuff the cavity of the bird using your hands or a long-

handled spoon. Save some stuffing to tuck under the neck flap to plump it.

6. Sew the cavity of the bird closed, or use skewers to secure it. Tie the legs together but do not cross them over. Tuck the neck skin under the wing tips and, if desired, use a trussing needle and fine string to secure them.

7. Place the turkey on a rack, breast side up, in a roasting pan. Soften the butter and spread some over the breast and the legs. Place the turkey in a preheated 325°F oven and cover loosely with foil. Roast for about 2 hours, basting often.

8. Remove the foil and continue roasting for another 2-2½ hours, or until the internal temperature in the thickest part of the thigh registers 350°F. Alternatively, pierce the thigh with a skewer – if the juices run clear then the turkey is done. Allow to rest for about 15-20 minutes before carving. Make gravy with the pan juices if desired and serve.

Step 8 Pierce the thigh with a skewer. The turkey is done when the juices run clear.

Cook's Notes

 Time
Preparation takes about 25-30 minutes and cooking takes about 4-4½ hours.

 Cook's Tip
Leaving a turkey or other roast bird to stand for 15-20 minutes before carving keeps the natural juices in the meat.

 Serving Idea
Don't save this just for Thanksgiving – serve with a selection of vegetables for a perfect family meal anytime.

DUCK IN CAPER SAUCE

A sweet-sour sauce with the tang of capers is a perfect
accompaniment to a rich meat such as duck.

1½-lb whole duck, giblets removed
1 clove garlic, crushed
Salt and pepper
1 tbsp oil
3 tbsps butter or margarine
1 cup chicken stock
½ cup water
4 tbsps sugar
1 tbsp vinegar or lemon juice
4 tsps cornstarch mixed with 2 tbsps water
6 tbsps capers

1. Rub the cavity of the duck with the crushed garlic and sprinkle in salt and pepper. Leave to stand 1-2 hours but do not refrigerate.

2. Heat the oil in a heavy skillet or roasting pan over a medium heat and when hot add the butter or margarine. Prick the duck skin all over with a sharp fork and brown the duck on all sides in the butter and oil. Transfer the duck to a saucepan or flameproof casserole.

3. Pour over the stock, cover and simmer over medium heat for about 1 hour 40 minutes, or until the duck is tender.

4. Meanwhile, heat the water and sugar together slowly in a small, heavy-based saucepan over a low heat until the sugar dissolves.

5. Once the sugar has dissolved, turn up the heat to high and allow the syrup to boil rapidly until it caramelizes. Remove from the heat and pour in the vinegar or lemon juice. It will splutter. Add several spoonfuls of the cooking liquid from the duck and set the caramel over medium heat. Allow mixture to come to the boil, stirring constantly.

Step 2 Brown the duck in a mixture of oil and butter over medium heat.

Step 4 Combine the sugar and the water in a heavy-based saucepan and cook to dissolve the sugar and make a clear syrup.

6. When the duck is tender, remove it to a heated serving dish. Skim off the fat from the cooking liquid and discard. Mix the water and cornstarch together and add several spoonfuls of the duck cooking liquid. Return to the rest of the liquid and bring to the boil. Add the capers and stir over high heat until the sauce clears and thickens. Add the caramel and stir until the sauce is thick.

7. Cut the duck into portions or serve whole and spoon over some of the sauce. Serve the rest of the sauce separately.

Cook's Notes

Time
Preparation takes about 20 minutes with 1-2 hours standing time for the duck. Cooking takes about 1 hour 50 minutes.

Cook's Tip
Pricking the duck skin with a sharp fork allows the fat to run out as the duck cooks. Use this method when roasting or pot roasting to produce duck that is not fatty.

Serving Idea
Serve with noodles and a green salad, instead of the more usual vegetables.

DUCK WITH ORANGES

This traditional combination is given extra flavor by cooking
the duck in a distinctly oriental manner.

3 oranges
1 duck
1 tbsp butter
1¼ tbsps oil
1¼ cups light chicken stock
⅓ cup red wine
2½ tbsps redcurrant jelly
Salt and pepper
1¼ tsps arrowroot
1¼ tbsps cold water

1. Using a potato peeler, carefully pare the rind thinly off two of the oranges.

Step 2 Using a sharp knife, carefully cut the pared orange rind into very thin strips.

2. Cut the rind into very fine shreds using a sharp knife. Put the shredded orange rind into a small bowl and cover with boiling water. Set aside to blanch for 5 minutes, then drain.

3. Squeeze the juice from the two oranges. Set this aside.

4. Cut away the peel and the pith from the remaining orange and then slice the flesh into thin rounds. Set aside.

5. Wash the duck and dry well with paper towels.

6. Put the butter and the oil into a large wok and heat until melted over a medium heat. Add the duck and cook, turning frequently, until it is brown all over.

7. Remove the duck from the wok, cool slightly and using poultry shears, cut away the leg and wing ends. Cut the duck in half lengthwise and then cut each half into 1-inch strips.

8. Remove the fat from the wok and return the duck to the wok. Add the stock, red wine, redcurrant jelly, squeezed orange juice, and the well drained strips of rind. Bring to the boil, then season to taste. Reduce the heat to low, cover

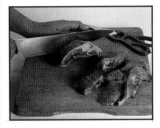

Step 7 Cut each half of the duck into 1-inch strips using poultry shears or a very sharp knife.

the wok and simmer the duck for 20 minutes, or until well cooked.

9. Skim away any surface fat and thicken the sauce by mixing the arrowroot with the water and stirring into the wok. Bring the mixture back to the boil and simmer for a further 5 minutes, or until the sauce is thick.

10. Arrange the duck on a serving plate, pour over the sauce, and garnish with the orange slices.

Cook's Notes

	Time		**Cook's Tip**		**Serving Idea**
	Preparation takes 30 minutes, cooking takes about 35 minutes.		Cornstarch can be used in place of the arrowroot to thicken the sauce.		Use watercress as extra garnish. Serve with game chips (see garnish section).

ZITI WITH HAM AND ASPARAGUS

Popular pasta gets a new twist with this subtly different sauce.

12oz fresh asparagus
4oz cooked ham
Salt
2 tbsps butter or margarine
1 cup heavy cream
8oz ziti
1 tbsp oil
Shredded Parmesan cheese (optional)

5. Melt the butter in the sauté pan over a medium heat and add the asparagus and ham. Cook briefly to reduce the liquid, and add the cream. Bring to the boil and cook over a low heat for about 5 minutes to thicken the cream.

6. Meanwhile, cook the ziti in boiling salted water with 1 tbsp oil for about 10-12 minutes.

7. Drain the ziti and rinse under hot water. Toss in a colander to drain and mix with the sauce. Serve with shredded Parmesan cheese, if desired.

Step 1 Peel the asparagus stalks with a swivel vegetable peeler.

1. Using a swivel vegetable peeler, scrape the sides of the asparagus spears starting about 2 inches from the top. Cut off the ends of the spears about 1 inch from the bottom.

2. Cut the ham into strips about ½ inch thick.

3. Bring a sauté pan of water to the boil over a medium heat, adding a pinch of salt. Move the pan so it is half on and half off direct heat. Place in the asparagus spears so that the tips are off the heat. Cover the pan and bring back to the boil. Cook the asparagus spears for about 2 minutes. Drain and allow to cool.

4. Cut the asparagus into 1-inch lengths, leaving the tips whole.

Step 4 Cut ham and cooked asparagus into 1-inch lengths. Leave the asparagus tips whole.

Step 5 Boil the cream with the asparagus and ham for about 5 minutes to thicken.

Cook's Notes

 Time
Pasta takes 10-12 minutes to cook. Sauce takes about 8 minutes to cook. Preparation takes about 20 minutes.

Cook's Tip
If using frozen instead of fresh asparagus, do not peel or pre-cook.

 Serving Idea
May be served as a first course in smaller amounts.

FETTUCINE ESCARGOTS WITH LEEKS AND SUN-DRIED TOMATOES

6 sun-dried tomatoes or 6 fresh Italian plum tomatoes
14oz canned escargots (snails), drained
12oz fresh or dried whole-wheat fettucine (tagliatelle)
3 tbsps olive oil
2 cloves garlic, crushed
1 large or 2 small leeks, trimmed, split, well washed and finely sliced
6 oyster, shittake or other large mushrooms
4 tbsps chicken or vegetable stock
3 tbsps dry white wine
6 tbsps heavy cream
2 tsps chopped fresh basil
2 tsps chopped fresh parsley
Salt and pepper

1. If you cannot obtain store bought sun dried tomatoes, plum tomatoes can be dried at home. First, cut the tomatoes in half lengthwise.

2. Use a teaspoon or your finger to scoop out about half the seeds and juice. Press gently with your palm to flatten slightly. Sprinkle both sides with salt and place tomatoes, cut side up, on a rack over a baking pan.

3. Place in the oven on the lowest possible setting, with door ajar, if necessary, for 24 hours, checking after 12 hours. Allow to dry until no liquid is left and the tomatoes are firm. Chop roughly. If using store-bought sun-dried tomatoes, simply chop roughly.

4. Drain the escargots well and dry with paper towels.

5. Place the fettucine in boiling salted water and cook for about 10-12 minutes, or until al dente. Drain, rinse under hot water and leave in a colander to drain.

6. Meanwhile, heat the olive oil in a skillet over a low-medium heat and add the garlic and leeks. Cook slowly to soften slightly, add the mushrooms and cook until the leeks are tender crisp. Remove to a plate. Add the drained escargots to the pan and cook over high heat for about 2 minutes, stirring constantly.

7. Pour on the stock and wine and bring to the boil over a high heat. Boil to reduce by about a quarter and add the cream and tomatoes. Bring to the boil then reduce the heat to low and cook slowly for about 3 minutes. Add the herbs, salt and pepper to taste. Add the leeks, mushrooms and fettucine to the pan and heat through thoroughly. Serve immediately.

Step 3 Properly dried tomatoes will look and feel firm, with no remaining liquid.

Cook's Notes

Time Preparation takes about 24 hours for the tomatoes to dry and about 15-20 minutes to finish the dish.	**Cook's Tip** Escargots are not to everyone's taste, so substitute more mushrooms, cooked shrimp or spicy sausage, as desired.	**Serving Idea** Serve as an appetizer or a main course with salad and bread. Shredded Parmesan cheese may be sprinkled on top, if desired.

SERVES 4
NOODLE STIR-FRY

Easy to prepare, this makes for a delicious, spicy Oriental-style meal.

8oz fine egg noodles
4 tbsps peanut oil
1 onion, finely chopped
2 cloves garlic, crushed
1 green chili pepper, seeded and finely sliced
1 tsp chili paste
4oz pork, finely sliced
2 celery stalks, sliced
¼ small cabbage, finely shredded
1 tbsp light soy sauce
¾ cup cooked shrimp, peeled and deveined
Salt and pepper

Step 1 Soak the noodles in hot water for 8 minutes, until they are soft. Rinse in cold water and drain thoroughly in a colander.

Step 4 Stir-fry the pork, celery and cabbage with the onion mixture for 3 minutes, or until the pork is cooked through.

1. Soak the noodles in hot water for 8 minutes, until they are soft. Rinse in cold water and drain thoroughly in a colander.

2. Heat the oil in a wok over a medium heat, and stir-fry the onion, garlic and chili pepper, until the onion is soft and just golden brown.

3. Add the chili paste and stir in well.

4. Add the pork, celery and cabbage to the cooked onions, and stir-fry for about 3 minutes, or until the pork is cooked through. Season to taste.

5. Stir in the soy sauce, noodles and shrimp, tossing the mixture together thoroughly and heating through before serving.

Cook's Notes

Time
Preparation takes about 20 minutes, and cooking takes about 15 minutes.

Cook's Tip
Great care should be taken when preparing green chili peppers. Try not to get juice into the eyes or mouth. If this should happen, rinse well with lots of cold water.

Serving Idea
Serve with plain boiled rice and shrimp crackers.

MACARONI AND CHEESE WITH FRANKFURTERS

8 frankfurter sausages
1lb macaroni
¼ cup butter or margarine
¾ cup all-purpose flour
2 cups milk
1½ cups Cheddar cheese, shredded
1 tsp dry mustard powder
Salt and pepper

Step 2 Remove the skins from the frankfurters and when they are completely cold, cut them diagonally into slices about 1-inch long.

1. Poach the frankfurters for 5-6 minutes in slightly salted boiling water.

2. Remove the skins from the frankfurters and, when cold, slice the meat diagonally.

3. Cook the macaroni in plenty of boiling salted water for about 20 minutes, or until tender.

4. Rinse in cold water and drain well.

5. Melt the butter in a saucepan over a medium heat. Stir in the flour and cook for 1 minute.

6. Remove the pan from the heat and add the milk gradually, beating thoroughly and returning the pan to the heat to cook between additions. When all the milk has been added, simmer over a low heat for 2 minutes, stirring occasionally.

7. Stir the frankfurters, shredded cheese and mustard into the sauce mixture. Season to taste.

Step 6 Add the milk gradually to the melted butter and flour mixture, reheating and beating the mixture well between additions, until all the milk is incorporated and the sauce is thick and smooth.

8. Add the drained macaroni to the sauce and frankfurter mixture, and stir well until heated through.

9. Pour the mixture into an ovenproof dish and top with a little extra shredded cheese, if desired.

10. Brown the dish under a preheated, medium broiler, until golden.

Cook's Notes

 Time
Preparation takes about 10 minutes, and cooking takes about 20 minutes.

 Cook's Tip
As a variation, use 6oz of chopped broiled or fried bacon in place of the frankfurters.

Serving Idea
To serve, make a lattice of sweet red pepper strips (see garnish section) over the top of the dish before broiling, and serve with a mixed salad.

LASAGNE ROLLS

These rolls, with their delicious creamy filling, make an interesting change from the more usual layered lasagne dishes.

Step 5 Melt half the butter in a large skillet and add the mushrooms and chicken. Cook these quickly, stirring continuously until the chicken is cooked, about 6-8 minutes.

---

2 tsps vegetable oil
8 lasagne sheets
½ cup button mushrooms, sliced
8oz boned chicken breast
2 tbsps butter or margarine
¼ cup all-purpose flour
½ cup milk
1 cup Gruyère or Cheddar cheese, shredded
Salt and pepper

---

1. Fill a large saucepan two thirds full with salted water. Add the oil and bring to the boil over a medium heat.

2. Add 1 sheet of lasagne, wait about 2 minutes, then add another sheet. Cook only a few at a time and when tender, after about 6-7 minutes, remove from the boiling water and rinse under cold water. Allow to drain.

3. Repeat this process until all the lasagne is cooked.

4. Wash and slice the mushrooms, and slice the chicken breast into thin strips.

5. Melt half the butter in a small skillet over a medium heat and cook the mushrooms and the chicken.

6. In a small saucepan, melt the rest of the butter over a medium heat. Stir in the flour and cook for 1 minute.

7. Remove the pan from the heat and add the milk gradually to the melted butter and flour mixture, stirring well and returning the pan to the heat between additions, to thicken the sauce.

8. Beat the sauce well and cook for 3 minutes over a low heat, until it is thick and smooth.

9. Pour the sauce into the skillet with the chicken and the

Step 11 Spread the chicken mixture evenly over each sheet of lasagne and roll up jelly roll fashion, starting from a narrow end.

mushrooms. Add half the cheese and mix well to incorporate thoroughly. Season to taste.

10. Lay the sheets of lasagne on a board and divide the chicken mixture equally between them.

11. Spread the chicken mixture evenly over each lasagne sheet and roll up lengthwise, like a jelly roll.

12. Put the rolls into an ovenproof dish. Sprinkle with the remaining cheese and broil under a preheated medium broiler, until the cheese is bubbly and golden brown.

Cook's Notes

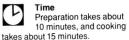 **Time**
Preparation takes about 10 minutes, and cooking takes about 15 minutes.

Cook's Tip
Pre-cooked lasagne is now widely available at most supermarkets and does not require initial cooking. If available, try preparing the dish with sheets of fresh lasagne, which also requires no pre-cooking.

 Serving Idea
Serve piping hot with a fresh green salad and crusty French bread.

ZITI WITH SPICY CHILI SAUCE

Ziti are hollow pasta tubes which can be bought at most supermarkets. Macaroni can be used equally as well. The sauce is fairly fiery and can be moderated by using only one red chili pepper.

1lb canned plum tomatoes
1 tbsp olive oil
2 cloves garlic, crushed
1 onion, chopped
4 strips bacon, chopped
2 red chili peppers, seeded and chopped
2 green onions, chopped
½ cup Pecorino or Parmesan cheese, shredded
1lb ziti or macaroni
Salt and pepper

1. Chop the tomatoes and sieve them to remove the pips.

2. Heat the oil in a skillet and cook the garlic, onion and bacon over a low heat for 6-8 minutes.

3. Add the sieved tomatoes, the chili peppers, chopped green onions and half of the cheese. Simmer over a low heat for 20 minutes.

4. Cook the ziti or macaroni in boiling, salted water for 10-15 minutes, or until tender. Rinse under hot water and drain well.

5. Put the cooked ziti or macaroni into a warm serving dish and toss it in half of the sauce. Pour the remaining sauce over the top and sprinkle with the remaining cheese.

Step 3 Stir the sieved tomatoes, chili peppers, green onions and half the cheese into the onion mixture.

Step 5 Toss the cooked ziti or macaroni in half of the sauce, mixing together well to coat evenly.

Cook's Notes

Time
Preparation takes about 15 minutes, and cooking takes about 40 minutes.

Cook's Tip
The sauce for this recipe will freeze for up to 2 months.

Serving Idea
Garnish the serving dish with green onion flowers (see garnish section) and serve with a mixed green salad.

46

SAN FRANCISCO RICE

This rice and pasta dish has been popular for a long time in
San Francisco, where it was invented.

4oz uncooked long grain rice
4oz uncooked spaghetti, broken into 2-inch pieces
3 tbsps oil
4 tbsps sesame seeds
2 tbsps chopped chives
Salt and pepper
1½ cups stock
1 tbsp soy sauce
2 tbsps chopped parsley

1. Rinse the rice and pasta to remove starch, and leave to drain dry.

2. Heat the oil in a large skillet and add the dried rice and pasta. Cook over a medium heat to brown the rice and pasta, stirring continuously.

3. Add the sesame seeds and cook until the rice, pasta and seeds are golden brown.

4. Add the chives, salt and pepper, and pour over 1 cup of the stock. Stir in the soy sauce and bring to the boil.

5. Cover and cook over a low heat about 20 minutes, or until the rice and pasta are tender and the stock is absorbed. Add more of the reserved stock as necessary. Do not let the rice and pasta dry out during cooking.

6. Fluff up the grains of rice with a fork and sprinkle with the parsley before serving.

Step 2 Cook the rice and pasta in the oil until just beginning to brown.

Step 3 Add the sesame seeds and cook until the rice, pasta and seeds are golden brown.

Step 5 Cook until all the liquid is absorbed and the pasta and rice are tender.

Cook's Notes

Time
Preparation takes about 25 minutes and cooking takes about 20 minutes or more.

Cook's Tip
If desired, once the stock is added the mixture may be cooked in a preheated 375°F oven. Cook for about 20 minutes, checking the level of liquid occasionally and adding more stock if necessary.

Serving Idea
Serve as a side dish with meat or poultry. Give it an Italian flavor by omitting sesame seeds, chives and soy sauce. Substitute Parmesan cheese and basil instead.

SERVES 6-8

SPICY RICE AND BEANS

A lively side dish or vegetarian main course, this recipe readily
takes to creative variations and even makes a good cold
salad.

4 tbsps oil
2 cups long grain rice
1 onion, finely chopped
1 green pepper, seeded and chopped
1 tsp each ground cumin and coriander
1-2 tsps Tabasco sauce
Salt
3½ cups stock
1lb canned red kidney beans, drained and rinsed
1lb canned tomatoes, drained and coarsely chopped
Chopped parsley

3. Add the Tabasco, salt, stock and beans and bring to the
boil. Cover and cook about 45 minutes, or until the rice is
tender and most of the liquid is absorbed.

4. Remove from the heat and add the tomatoes, stirring
them in gently. Leave to stand, covered, for 5 minutes.

5. Fluff up the mixture with a fork and sprinkle with parsley
to serve.

Step 2 Cook the rice
in the oil until just
turning opaque.

Step 3 Cook with
the remaining
ingredients until rice
is tender and most
of the liquid is
absorbed

Step 4 Carefully stir
in the tomatoes
before covering and
leaving to stand.

1. Heat the oil in a casserole or a large, deep saucepan
over a low heat.

2. Add the rice and cook until just turning opaque. Add the
onion, pepper and cumin and coriander. Cook gently for a
further 2 minutes.

Cook's Notes

 Time
Preparation takes about
25 minutes and cooking
takes about 50 minutes.

 Cook's Tip
The recipe may be made
with 1lb fresh tomatoes,
peeled, seeded and coarsely
chopped.

Serving Idea
Serve with warm tortillas
and a salad for a light
vegetarian meal. Serve as a side
dish with enchiladas, meat or poultry,
or cheese and egg dishes.

SERVES 6-8

RED BEANS AND RICE

Served every Monday in New Orleans, this is a delicious way
of making a small amount of meat go a long way.

8oz dried red kidney beans
1 sprig thyme
1 bay leaf
8oz ham or bacon
¼ cup butter or margarine
1 onion, finely chopped
1 green pepper, seeded and cut into small dice
3 celery stalks, finely chopped
2 cloves garlic, crushed
1 tsp cayenne pepper
Salt
8oz rice, cooked
4 green onions, finely chopped

---

1. Pick over the beans and place them in a large stock-pot or bowl. Cover with water and leave to soak overnight. Drain them and place in a pot of fresh water with the sprig of thyme, bay leaf and a pinch of salt. Add the piece of ham or bacon and bring to the boil. Partially cover the pan and leave to boil rapidly over a high heat for 10 minutes. Re-

duce the heat to low and then simmer for 2½-3 hours, adding more water if necessary.

2. When the beans have been cooking for about half the required length of time, melt the butter in a small skillet over a medium heat and cook the onion, pepper, garlic and celery until the onions look translucent. Add this mixture to the beans and continue cooking.

3. Once the beans are soft, mash some of them against the side of the pot with a large spoon. Alternatively, remove about ¾ cup of the mixture and blend to a smooth purée in a food processor or blender. Pour back into the pot to thicken the rest of the beans.

4. Remove the piece of ham or bacon, trim off excess fat and cut the meat into ½-inch pieces. Return to the beans and add cayenne pepper. Stir well and continue to cook the beans. Remove thyme and bay leaf before serving.

5. To serve, place the hot, cooked rice on serving plates and spoon over some of the beans. Sprinkle the top with the chopped green onion.

Step 1 Soak the kidney beans in water overnight, until they swell in size.

Step 3 Once the beans are completely softened, mash some of them against the side of the pot with a large spoon.

Cook's Notes

Time
Preparation takes about 25 minutes, with overnight soaking for the beans. Cooking takes about 2½-3 hours.

Serving Idea
Serve with tortilla chips and a green salad.

Cook's Tip
The beans must boil vigorously for the first 10 minutes of cooking time. Make sure that the beans are completely cooked – it can be dangerous to eat dried pulses that are insufficiently cooked.

49

SPICED CHICK-PEAS

This very fragrant, fairly mild curry is delicious on its own, or as part of a larger Indian meal.

1lb chick-peas, soaked overnight in cold water
3 tbsps oil
1 large onion, chopped
2 bay leaves
2 green chili peppers, sliced in half lengthwise
1-inch piece cinnamon stick
1-inch piece fresh root ginger, shredded
4 cloves garlic, crushed
1½ tsps ground coriander
4 cloves, ground
1 tsp cumin seeds, ground
Seeds of 4 large black cardamoms, ground
Seeds of 4 small cardamoms, ground
10oz canned tomatoes, chopped
Salt and pepper
6 sprigs fresh coriander leaves, chopped

1. Cook the chick-peas over a medium heat in their soaking water, until they are soft. Drain and reserve 1 cup of the cooking liquid.

2. Heat the oil in a skillet over a low-medium heat and cook the onion gently, until soft, but not colored. Add the bay leaves, chili peppers, cinnamon, ginger and garlic and cook for a further 1 minute.

3. Stir in the ground spices, the tomatoes and a generous amount of salt and pepper.

4. Add the reserved cooking liquid and the drained chick-peas. Mix well. Sprinkle with the chopped coriander leaves, cover and simmer for 10 minutes, adding a little extra liquid if necessary.

Step 1 Cook the chick-peas in their soaking water.

Step 2 Cook the bay leaves, chili peppers, cinnamon, ginger and garlic with the onion for 1 minute.

Step 4 Mix the chick-peas thoroughly into the spicy sauce.

Cook's Notes

 Time
Preparation takes about 15 minutes, plus overnight soaking. Cooking takes about 45-50 minutes.

 **Cook's Tip**
Add 1 tsp of baking powder to the chick-peas when soaking overnight, to make them really tender. The chick-peas can be cooked in a pressure cooker for 10-15 minutes.

Serving Idea
Serve with slices of whole-wheat bread or lightly curried rice and chutney.

MAIN COURSES

A well-made garnish enhances a dish, ensuring that it appeals to the eye and also whets the appetite. Wherever possible, garnishes should reflect a dish's ingredients, e.g. Fish, Zucchini and Lemon Kebabs uses lemon, which therefore suggests itself as the garnish in some form.

CARROT FLOWERS

Use a carrot that is thick and large, rather than thin and pointed. Trim the ends, and peel the carrot.

Using a sharp knife, cut rings into the carrot in "V" shapes into the carrot all along its length. Cut across the carrot between the rings of "V"s to make flowers.

CHILI FLOWERS

Red or green chili peppers may be prepared as green onion flowers, but care should be taken to remove the seeds and to prevent the chili from coming into contact with the skin and eyes – always wash hands thoroughly after preparation. Chili flowers do look very pretty and are well worth making. The chili peppers require soaking for at least 4 hours, before they curl open.

GAME CHIPS

These are a good garnish for roast poultry and game, and for steaks and chops. Peel potatoes and, using a sharp knife, slice them very thinly and evenly. Soak the potato slices in cold water to remove the

starch, then drain and dry thoroughly on paper towels. Cook in hot oil for 2-3 minutes until golden brown. Drain on paper towels and serve immediately.

GHERKIN FANS

These are best used to garnish cold meats and salamis, hors d'oeuvres and cheese boards. Using a sharp knife, cut through the gherkin from the pointed end at regular intervals, keeping it joined at the stem end. Gently spread the slices apart to form a fan.

GREEN ONION FLOWERS

Trim the green top, and remove any leaves that are damaged. Cut off the white part to about ¾ inch-1 inch from the base of the green leaves. Carefully shred the green top into fine strips, without

CUCUMBER FANS

These are particularly good as a garnish for either whole cold fish or Chinese dishes. Cut a 3-inch piece from the rounded end of

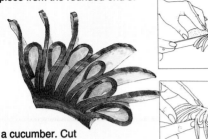

a cucumber. Cut this in half lengthwise. Cut each half into strips to within ½ inch of the end, then trim each strip, cutting away the excess flesh to about ¼ inch thick. Carefully trim alternate strips up to the uncut end.

CUTLET FRILLS

These are used to decorate any exposed bones, such as on chicken drumsticks or lamb cutlets. Use a piece of plain white paper 10 inches long by 3½ inches wide. Fold the paper lengthwise to within ½ inch of the top of the paper. Make a series of closely-spaced cuts through the

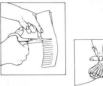

folded edge along the length of the paper. Open out the strip and refold, inside out, lining up the long edges. Fold back ½ inch to form a cuff. Cut to the desired length, which will be larger for poultry than for cutlets, and carefully roll into a frill, with the cuff outside. Secure with tape. Place onto the cooked meat just before serving.

detaching it. The green onion will resemble a tassel. Immerse in iced water for about 1 hour, until the top curls open.

LEMON AND CUCUMBER CONES

Thinly slice lemons and cucumbers. Make an incision from the center to the edge of each slice.

Hold each side and twist to form a cone. Slices of cucumber and lemon may be twisted together to make a double cone of green and yellow.

TURNED CARROTS, TURNIPS AND POTATOES

Trim and peel the vegetables, and cut into even-sized pieces. Holding each one between the thumb and forefinger, cut it into a barrel shape, tapering it at the top and bottom, turning the vegetable as you go. Cook in the usual way and toss in butter before serving.

TURNED MUSHROOMS

Choose even-sized button mushrooms and, using a small, sharp knife, score the cap from the center to the edge,

removing a little flesh each time. Cook in butter or oil before serving.

TURNED VEGETABLES

Turned mushrooms, carrots and zucchini are an excellent garnish for roast meat, poultry and game.

DESERTS

CONTENTS

CRANBERRY SNOW WITH MINT

Cranberries are usually associated with turkey at
Thanksgiving. However, because these delicious berries have
an interesting flavor, they can also be used to make some mouthwatering desserts.

½ cup fresh or frozen cranberries
2 tbsps granulated sugar
2 egg whites
4 tbsps superfine sugar
½ cup whipping cream
½ cup plain yogurt
2 tbsps chopped fresh mint

glossy and form stiff peaks.

6. Whip the cream until it is thick and combine this with the yogurt in a large bowl.

7. Fold the egg whites carefully into the cream and yogurt mixture.

8. Stir in the cooked, cooled cranberries and the chopped mint. Do not over-mix, as the dessert should look marbled.

9. Spoon into individual serving dishes.

Step 2 Cook the cranberries slowly, until the juice runs and the fruit softens. Set the berries aside to cool completely.

Step 5 Beat the superfine sugar gradually into the beaten egg whites. Beat well between each addition of sugar, until stiff peaks form and the egg whites are smooth and glossy.

1. Put the cranberries and the granulated sugar into a small, heavy-based pan.

2. Cook the cranberries slowly over a moderate heat, until they soften and the juice begins to run.

3. Set the cranberries aside to cool completely.

4. Beat the egg whites with a whisk until they are stiff, but not dry.

5. Gradually beat in the superfine sugar, beating well between additions, until the egg whites are smooth and

Step 8 Fold the cooled cooked cranberries and the chopped mint lightly into the egg white and cream mixture. Do not over-mix, as the finished dish should look marbled.

Cook's Notes

Time
Preparation takes about 15 minutes, and cooking takes about 5 minutes.

Cook's Tip
Any kind of soft fruit can be used instead of cranberries in this recipe.

Serving Idea
Serve decorated with whole sprigs of frosted mint leaves (see decoration section) and crisp cookies.

COFFEE PECAN PIE

Sumptuous and rich, this traditional American pie is ideal for
serving afer a celebration meal.

6oz graham crackers
4 tbsps margarine, melted
1½ cups pecan nut halves
6oz marshmallows
1 cup strong decaffeinated black coffee
½oz gelatin
3 tbsps hot water
1 egg white
½ cup fromage frais, or sour cream

1. Crush the cookies into fine crumbs and mix together with the melted butter.

2. Press the crumb mixture onto the base and halfway up the sides of a well-greased 7-inch, spring-form cake pan. Chill the cookie crumb base for at least 1 hour.

3. Reserve some pecan nut halves for decoration, and chop the remainder finely.

4. In a large saucepan, dissolve the marshmallows in the coffee, by heating over a low heat and stirring frequently.

5. Sprinkle the gelatin onto the hot water and stir, until it is clear and has dissolved completely.

6. Carefully pour the gelatin into the marshmallow mixture, and stir well, to ensure that it is evenly mixed in. Leave the coffee and marshmallow mixture to cool, until it is almost set. Beat the egg white with a whisk until it forms soft peaks, and fold this carefully into the fromage frais.

8. Fold the fromage frais into the coffee and marshmallow mixture with a metal spoon, incorporating as much air as possible, and making sure that the fromage frais is evenly blended.

9. Stir in the chopped nuts and pour the mixture onto the chilled base.

10. Chill the pie in the refrigerator for at least 4 hours, until completely set.

11. Remove the sides of the pan, and slide the pie carefully onto a serving dish. Decorate with the reserved nut halves.

Step 3 Reserve some of the nuts for decoration and chop the remainder finely.

Step 4 Put the marshmallows and the coffee into a large saucepan, and heat gently, stirring, until the marshmallows have completely dissolved.

Cook's Notes

Time
Preparation takes about 20 minutes, plus at least 4 hours' chilling time.

Cook's Tip
To remove the cake from the pan, run a round-bladed knife, which has previously been dipped into boiling water, carefully around the edge, to loosen the sides.

Serving Idea
Decorate with a few coffee beans. For a party, serve in smaller slices with ice cream to feed 10-12 people.

TIRAMISU

A luxurious dessert for special occasions.

2 tbsps cornstarch
2 cups milk
2 eggs, lightly beaten
2 tbsps sugar
Grated rind of ½ lemon
Pinch nutmeg
1 punnet ripe strawberries
16 ladyfingers
Amaretto
½ cup heavy cream

Step 1 Combine the custard ingredients in a heavy-based saucepan and cook until the mixture thickens and comes to the boil.

1. Mix the cornstarch with some of the milk. Beat the eggs, sugar, lemon rind and nutmeg together and pour in the remaining milk. Mix with the cornstarch mixture in a heavy-based pan and stir over a low heat until the mixture thickens and comes to the boil.

2. Allow to boil for 1 minute or until the mixture coats the back of a spoon. Place a sheet of wax paper directly on top of the custard and allow it to cool slightly.

Step 3 Place a layer of ladyfingers and strawberries in a serving dish and coat with a layer of custard. Repeat with remaining ingredients.

3. Save some even-sized strawberries for decoration and hull the remaining ones. Place half of the ladyfingers in the bottom of a glass bowl and sprinkle with some of the amaretto. Cut the strawberries in half and place a layer on top of the ladyfingers. Pour a layer of custard on top and repeat with the remaining sliced strawberries and ladyfingers. Top with another layer of custard and allow to cool completely.

Step 4 Decorate the top using a pastry bag fitted with a rosette tube.

4. Whip the cream and spread a thin layer over the top of the set custard. Pipe the remaining cream around the edge of the dish and decorate with the reserved strawberries. Serve chilled.

Cook's Notes

Time
Preparation takes about 20 minutes, custard takes about 5 minutes to cook.

Cook's Tip
It is important to keep stirring the custard as it comes to the boil, to prevent lumps forming.

Serving Idea
Decorate the top of the dessert with grated chocolate, toasted almonds or shelled pistachios in addition to, or instead of, the strawberries.

MEXICAN MANGO FOOL

To cool the palate after a spicy Mexican meal, the taste of
mango, lime, ginger and cream is perfect.

2 ripe mangoes
1 small piece fresh ginger, peeled and shredded
1 cup powdered sugar, sifted
Juice of ½ a lime
½ cup heavy cream

Step 1 Cut the mango in half, slicing around the stone. Scoop out pulp.

Step 3 Whip the cream to soft peaks.

Step 3 Fold the cream into the mango purée using a large spoon or rubber spatula.

1. Cut the mangoes in half, slicing around the stone. Scoop out the pulp into a bowl, blender or food processor. Reserve two slices.

2. Add the ginger, powdered sugar and lime juice and purée in the blender or food processor until smooth. Use a hand-held blender or electric mixer in the bowl, pushing mixture through a sieve afterwards, if necessary.

3. Whip the cream until soft peaks form and fold into the mango purée.

4. Divide the mixture between 6 glass serving dishes and leave in the refrigerator for 1 hour before serving.

5. Cut the reserved mango slices into 6 smaller slices or pieces and use to decorate the fool.

Cook's Notes

Time
Preparation takes about 20 minutes. Fool should be refrigerated 1 hour before serving.

Cook's Tip
When whipping cream, refrigerate it for at least 2 hours before use. Overwhipped cream turns to butter, so whip slowly and watch carefully.

Serving Idea
Accompany with cookies.

MAPLE SYRUP MOUSSE

Pure maple syrup is a true delicacy. It isn't cheap,
but the flavor it gives special recipes like this mousse
makes it worth its price.

¾ cup maple syrup
4 eggs, separated
2 extra egg whites
1 cup heavy cream
Chopped pecans or walnuts to decorate

1. Place the syrup in a saucepan and bring to the boil over a medium heat. Continue boiling to reduce the syrup by one quarter.

2. Beat the egg yolks until thick and lemon colored.

3. Pour the maple syrup onto the egg yolks in a thin, steady stream, beating with an electric mixer. Continue beating until the mixture has cooled.

4. Beat the egg whites with a whisk until stiff but not dry and whip the cream until soft peaks form.

5. Fold the cream and egg whites into the maple mixture and spoon into a serving bowl or individual glasses. Refrigerate until slightly set and top with chopped pecans or walnuts to serve.

Step 3 Pour the hot syrup onto the beaten egg yolks in a thin, steady stream, beating constantly.

Step 5 Fold the cream and the egg whites into the maple mixture using a rubber spatula or large metal spoon.

Cook's Notes

Time
Preparation takes about 30 minutes. It will take the syrup about 10 minutes to reduce.

Cook's Tip
Be careful when boiling the syrup, since it can burn very easily.

Serving Idea
Finely chopped pieces of maple sugar can be used instead of nuts to decorate the top of the mousse.

STAINED GLASS DESSERT

Named for the effect of the cubes of colorful gelatin in the filling, this pretty and light pudding can be made well in advance of serving.

Step 7 Fold the cubes of flavored gelatin carefully into the lemon-cheese mixure using a rubber spatula.

3oz each of three fruit flavored gelatins (assorted)
2 cups graham crackers, crushed
6 tbsps sugar
½ cup butter or margarine
3 tbsps unflavored gelatin
4 tbsps cold water
3 eggs, separated
Juice and rind 1 large lemon
6 tbsps sugar
4oz cream cheese
½ cup whipping cream

Step 8 Sprinkle reserved crumb topping carefully over the mixture and press down lightly.

1. Prepare the flavored gelatins according to package directions.

2. Pour into 3 shallow pans and refrigerate until firm.

3. Mix the crushed graham crackers with the sugar in a food processor and pour melted butter through the funnel with the machine running to blend thoroughly.

4. Press half the mixture into an 8-inch springform pan lined with wax paper. Refrigerate until firm. Reserve half the mixture for topping.

5. Sprinkle the unflavored gelatin onto the water in a small saucepan and allow to stand until spongy. Heat over a low heat until the gelatin dissolves and the liquid is clear. Combine the egg yolks, lemon juice and sugar and beat until slightly thickened. Beat in the cream cheese a bit at a time. Pour in the gelatin in a thin, steady stream, beating constantly. Allow to stand, stirring occasionally, until beginning to thicken. Place in a bowl of ice water to speed up the setting process.

6. Whip the cream until soft. Beat the egg whites with a

whisk until stiff peaks form and fold both the cream and the egg whites into the lemon-cream cheese mixture when the gelatin has begun to thicken.

7. Cut the flavored gelatins into cubes and fold carefully into the cream cheese mixture.

8. Pour onto the prepared crust. Sprinkle the remaining crust mixture on top, pressing down very carefully.

9. Chill overnight in the refrigerator. Loosen the mixture carefully from the sides of the pan, open the pan and unmold. Slice or spoon out to serve.

Cook's Notes

Time
Preparation takes about 35-40 minutes. Flavored gelatins will take about 1-1½ hours to set, and the finished cake must be refrigerated overnight.

Cook's Tip
Cake may be prepared a day or two in advance and kept in the refrigerator. Do not keep longer than 2 days.

Serving Idea
Serve with extra whipped cream for a sumptuous dessert.

CINNAMON CŒUR À LA CRÈME WITH RASPBERRY SAUCE

Delicious cinnamon creams are complemented delightfully by the sharp raspberry sauce.

1 cup cream cheese
1½ cups whipping cream
¾ cup powdered sugar, sifted
2½ tsps ground cinnamon
½lb fresh raspberries
⅛ cup powdered sugar

Step 5 Line four individual Cœur à la Crème molds with dampened cheesecloth, extending the material beyond the edges of the molds.

1. Put the cream cheese into a large bowl along with 5 tbsps of the cream. Whip with an electric mixer until the mixture is light and fluffy.

2. Mix in the ¾ cup of powdered sugar and the cinnamon, stirring well until all ingredients are well blended.

3. Whip the remaining cream in another bowl until it forms soft peaks.

4. Fold the cream into the cheese mixture with a metal spoon.

5. Line four individual Cœur à la Crème molds with dampened cheesecloth, extending the material beyond the edges of the molds.

6. Spoon the cheese mixture into the mold and spread out evenly, pressing down well to remove any air bubbles.

7. Fold the overlapping edges of the cheesecloth over the top of the mixture, and refrigerate the molds on a rack placed over a tray, for at least 8 hours.

8. Purée the raspberries in a blender or food processor and press through a nylon sieve to remove all the seeds.

Step 7 Stand the molds on a rack over a tray to collect the drips when refrigerated.

9. Blend the ⅛ cup of powdered sugar into the fruit purée to sweeten.

10. Carefully remove the cheesecloth from the cream cheese hearts, and place each one on a serving dish.

11. Spoon a little of the sauce over each heart and serve the remainder separately.

Cook's Notes

Time
Preparation takes 15 minutes, plus overnight refrigerating.

Cook's Tip
It is important to use proper Cœur à la Crème molds as these have small holes in the base which allow any excess liquid to drain off during the chilling time.

Serving Idea
Serve these cream cheese desserts with a little extra whipped cream and frosted rose petals (see decoration section).

RASPBERRY SOUFFLÉ

This light dessert is the perfect finale for a dinner party.

1lb raspberries
Liquid sweetener to taste
2 tbsps gelatin
⅔ cup hot water
4 eggs, separated
1¼ cups heavy cream

1. Prepare a 6-inch soufflé dish by tightly tying a lightly oiled sheet of wax paper carefully around the outside edge of the soufflé dish, allowing it to stand approximately 4 inches above the rim of the dish.

2. Reserve a few of the raspberries for decoration, and purée the remainder using a blender or food processor.

3. Rub the puréed raspberries through a nylon sieve to remove the hard pips.

4. Sweeten the smooth raspberry purée with the liquid sweetener and set aside.

5. Dissolve the gelatin in the hot water, stirring gently until it is completely dissolved and the liquid is clear.

6. Allow the gelatin to cool slightly and then beat it into the raspberry purée along with the egg yolks, mixing until all ingredients are well blended. Chill in the refrigerator until partially set.

7. Beat the egg whites with a whisk until they form soft peaks.

8. Lightly whip the cream until it just holds its shape.

9. Remove the partially set raspberry mixture from the refrigerator, and carefully fold in half the cream and the egg

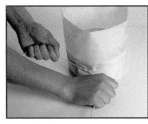

Step 1 Tie a sheet of wax paper around the soufflé dish, to form a collar rising above the rim of the dish.

Step 3 Press the raspberry purée through a sieve to remove the pips.

whites, blending lightly but thoroughly until the mixture is smooth.

10. Turn the soufflé mixture into the prepared dish, allowing it to rise about 1 inch above the rim of the dish inside the paper collar. Allow to set in the refrigerator.

11. When completely set, remove the collar carefully and decorate the soufflé with the remaining whipped cream and the reserved raspberries.

Cook's Notes

🕐 **Time**
Preparation takes about 40 minutes, plus chilling time.

🧑‍🍳 **Cook's Tip**
Take great care not to overmix the soufflé mixture when adding the egg whites, or there will not be enough to rise up over the rim of the dish inside the collar.

 Serving Idea
Accompany with a sweetened and sieved strawberry purée.

CHOCOLATE BRANDY MOUSSE

Chocolate and brandy blend together to create a delicious
mousse which sets to a rich cream in the refrigerator.

6oz unsweetened chocolate
5½ tbsps water
1¼ tbsps unsalted butter
3 eggs, separated
2½ tbsps brandy
5 tbsps grated chocolate

1. Break the unsweetened chocolate into small pieces
and place in a large bowl with the water.

2. Stand the bowl over a saucepan which has been half
filled with simmering water over a low heat. Stir the chocolate and water together until they melt and combine
thoroughly.

3. Remove the bowl from the saucepan and allow to cool
slightly.

4. Cut the butter into small dice and add this to the melted
chocolate, stirring it gently to blend it in as it melts.

5. Beat the egg yolks, one at a time, into the melted chocolate mixture, then stir in the brandy.

6. Put the egg whites into a large bowl and beat them with
an electric or hand whisk, until they are stiff, but not dry.

7. Fold these carefully into the chocolate mixture.

8. Divide the chocolate mousse between 6 serving dishes
and chill overnight before serving.

9. Sprinkle with grated chocolate to serve.

Step 2 Melt the
chocolate in a large
bowl placed over a
pan of simmering
water.

Step 7 Carefully fold
the beaten egg
whites into the
chocolate mixture
using a spatula or
metal spoon.

Cook's Notes

Time
Preparation takes
20 minutes, cooking takes
about 10 minutes.

Cook's Tip
Take great care not to melt
the chocolate too quickly or
it will separate.

Serving Idea
Make chocolate leaves (see
decoration section) to
decorate the mousses in place of the
grated chocolate.

HONEY PLUM COBBLER

This pudding derives its name from the 'cobbles' that the
scones arranged around the edge of the pudding are
supposed to represent.

2lbs ripe plums, halved and pitted
4-6 tbsps clear honey, to taste
2 cups whole-wheat self-rising flour
2 tbsps unrefined soft brown sugar
1 tbsp margarine
½ cup plain yogurt or fromage frais
Skim milk for glazing

1. Put the plums into an ovenproof dish with the honey. Cover the dish with a sheet of aluminum foil and cook in a preheated oven, 400°F, for 15 minutes.

2. Put the flour and sugar into a large mixing bowl and rub in the margarine with your fingertips.

3. Using a round-bladed knife or fork, stir the yogurt into the flour mixture, until it forms a soft, but firm, dough.

4. Lightly flour a pastry board, or work surface, and knead the dough until it is smooth.

Step 5 Cut 2-inch circles out of the dough with a cookie cutter, to form the cobbles.

Step 7 Arrange the scone cobbles around the edge of the dish, overlapping them slightly and brushing them with a little milk to glaze.

Step 3 Using a round-bladed knife or fork, stir the yogurt into the flour mixture until it forms a soft but firm dough.

5. Roll the dough out until it is approximately ¾ inch thick. Cut out rounds of dough using a 2-inch cutter, to form the cobbles.

6. Remove the plums from the oven and leave to cool.

7. Arrange the cobbles around the ege of the dish, over-lapping them slightly. Brush the top of each cobble with a little milk.

8. Return the dish to the oven and cook until the cobbles are well risen and brown.

Cook's Notes

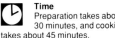

Time
Preparation takes about 30 minutes, and cooking takes about 45 minutes.

Cook's Tip
Use any fruit suitable for stewing, in place of the plums.

Serving Idea
Serve piping hot with spoonfuls of fromage frais or sour cream and a sprinkling of cinnamon or mixed spice.

BUCKWHEAT AND RAISIN PUDDING

Popular in East European cooking, buckwheat is a nutty,
protein-rich ingredient.

3 cups milk
1 vanilla pod
6 tbsps butter or margarine
1 cup buckwheat
4 eggs, separated
¾ cup sugar
1-1¼ cups raisins
Grated rind of half a lemon

1. Boil the milk with the vanilla pod in a large saucepan over a medium heat.

2. Stir in 4 tbsps of the butter until melted. Reserve remaining butter.

3. Pick over the buckwheat and add it to the milk, stirring well.

4. Cook, uncovered, over low heat, stirring occasionally to prevent sticking.

5. When the mixture thickens, transfer it to an ovenproof dish with a tight-fitting lid. Bake in a preheated 375°F oven

Step 6 Beat the egg yolks with the sugar until light and fluffy.

Step 7 Beat the egg whites just until stiff peaks form.

Step 2 Boil milk with the vanilla pod in a large saucepan and stir in 4 tbsps of the butter.

for 45 minutes. Remove the vanilla pod and allow the mixture to cool slightly.

6. Beat the egg yolks with the sugar until light and fluffy. Add lemon rind, mix with the buckwheat, and stir in the raisins.

7. Beat egg whites with a whisk until stiff peaks form and fold into the buckwheat mixture.

8. Smooth the top of the pudding and dot with the remaining butter. Bake a further 30 minutes at 375°F.

Cook's Notes

Time
Preparation takes about 20 minutes, cooking takes a total of 1 hour 25 minutes.

Cook's Tip
Vanilla pods and cinnamon sticks may be used several times. Rinse and dry after use and store air tight.

Serving Idea
Serve with a red-cherry sauce and/or cream.

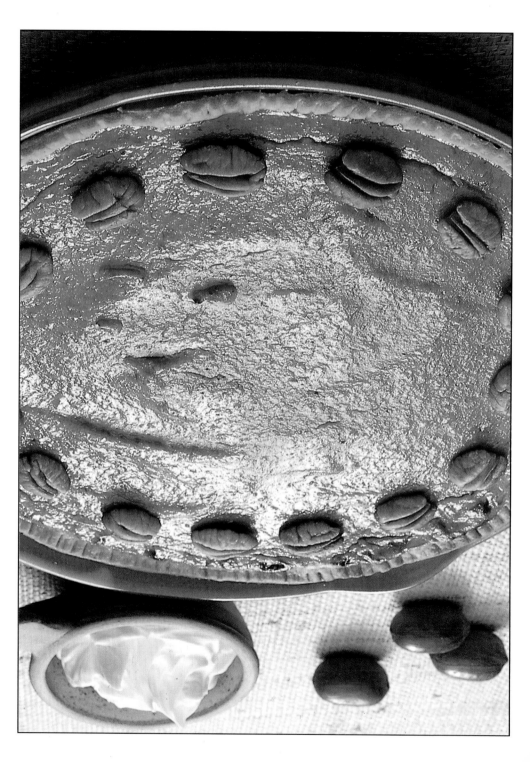

PUMPKIN PIE

Native Americans taught the settlers about the pumpkin and it
was one of the crops that helped to save their lives.

Pastry
1 cup all-purpose flour
Pinch salt
¼ cup butter or margarine
Cold milk

Pumpkin Filling
1lb cooked and mashed pumpkin
2 eggs
1 cup evaporated milk
½ cup brown sugar
1 tsp ground cinnamon
¼ tsp ground allspice
Pinch nutmeg
Pecan halves for decoration

Step 1 Add enough cold milk to bring the mixture together into a firm ball.

Step 3 Wrap the pastry around a lightly-floured rolling pin and then lower it into the dish.

Step 1 Rub the fat into the flour until the mixture resembles fine bread crumbs.

1. To prepare the pastry, sift the flour and a pinch of salt into a mixing bowl. Rub in the fat until the mixture resembles fine bread crumbs. Stir in enough cold milk to bring the mixture together into a firm ball. Cover and chill for about 30 minutes before use.

2. Roll out the pastry on a lightly-floured surface to a circle about 11 inches in diameter.

3. Wrap the pastry around a lightly-floured rolling pin and lower it into a 10-inch round pie dish.

4. Press the pastry into the dish and flute the edge or crimp with a fork.

5. Prick the base lightly with the tines of a fork.

6. Combine all the filling ingredients in a mixing bowl and beat with an electric mixer until smooth. Alternatively, use a food processor. Pour into the pie crust and bake in a pre-heated 425°F oven. Bake for 10 minutes at this temperature and then lower the temperature to 350°F and bake for a further 40-50 minutes, or until the filling is set. Decorate with a circle of pecan halves.

Cook's Notes

Time
Preparation takes about 30 minutes and cooking takes about 50-60 minutes.

Cook's Tip
Pricking the base of the pastry lightly will prevent it from rising up in an air bubble in the middle of the pie.

Serving Idea
Serve warm or cold with whipped cream.

BLUEBERRY PIE

Americans love pie for dessert. In New England, where blueberries flourish, it's only natural to find them in a pie.

Double quantity pastry for Pumpkin Pie recipe

Filling
1lb blueberries
2 tbsps cornstarch
4 tbsps water
2 tbsps lemon juice
1 cup sugar
1 egg beaten with a pinch of salt

1. Prepare the pastry as for the Pumpkin Pie recipe.

2. Divide the pastry in half and roll out one half to form the base. Use a floured rolling pin to lower it into the dish, and press it against the sides. Chill the pastry in the dish and the remaining half of the pastry while preparing the filling.

3. Place the fruit in a bowl and mix the cornstarch with the water and lemon juice. Pour it over the fruit, add the sugar and mix together gently.

4. Spoon the fruit filling into the pastry base.

5. Roll out the remaining pastry on a lightly-floured surface and cut it into strips.

6. Use the strips to make a lattice pattern on top of the filling and press the edges to stick them to the pastry base. Cut off any excess pastry.

7. Using your fingers or a fork, crimp edges to decorate.

8. Brush the crimped edge of the pastry and the lattice strips lightly with the beaten egg and bake in a preheated 425°F oven for about 10 minutes. Reduce the heat to 350°F and bake for a further 40-45 minutes. Serve warm or cold.

Step 4 Spoon the blueberry filling into the pastry-lined pie dish.

Step 6 Cut strips of pastry and use to make a lattice pattern on top of the pie.

Step 7 Crimp by hand, or use a fork to make a decorative edge.

 *Cook's Notes*

 **Time**
Preparation takes about 30-40 minutes and cooking takes about 50-55 minutes.

Cook's Tip
Taste the blueberries before deciding how much sugar to add – it may not be necessary to add the full amount.

 Serving Idea
Serve with ice cream.

STEAMED CRANBERRY PUDDING WITH CITRUS SAUCE

Colonial women brought their favorite recipes with them and learned to adapt them to the local produce, hence an English steamed pudding with American cranberries.

1½ cups all-purpose flour
2 tsps baking powder
Pinch salt
1 cup chopped cranberries
1 small piece candied ginger, finely chopped
2 eggs, well beaten
½ cup honey
6 tbsps milk
Orange sauce
½ cup sugar
1 tbsp cornstarch
Grated juice and rind of 1 orange
Grated juice and rind of ½ lemon
¾ cup water
1 tbsp butter or margarine

1. Sift the dry ingredients together in a large bowl.

2. Toss in the cranberries and ginger.

3. Mix the eggs, honey and milk together and gradually stir into the dry ingredients and the cranberries. Do not over stir. The mixture should not be uniformly pink but should be of thick dropping consistency. Add more milk if necessary.

4. Spoon the mixture into a well-buttered pudding basin or bowl, cover with buttered foil and tie the top securely.

5. Place the bowl on a rack in a pan of boiling water to come halfway up the sides. Cover the pan and steam the pudding over a low heat for about 1½ hours, or until a skewer inserted into the center comes out clean. Leave to cool in the basin or bowl for about 10 minutes, loosen the edge with a knife and turn out onto a plate.

6. Meanwhile, place the sugar and cornstarch into a saucepan with the orange juice and rind and lemon juice and rind. Add the water, stirring to blend well. Bring to the boil over a low heat, stirring continuously and allow to simmer until clear. Beat in the butter at the end and serve with the pudding.

Step 3 Stir the liquid ingredients into the dry until well blended and of thick dropping consistency.

Step 4 Spoon into the prepared bowl or basin. Cover the top with foil and tie securely with string.

Cook's Notes

Time
Preparation takes about 30-40 minutes and cooking takes about 1½ hours.

Cook's Tip
Ground ginger can be used instead of the candied ginger.

Serving Idea
Serve with whipped cream flavored with a little candied ginger syrup instead of the orange sauce.

CRÊPES À L'ORANGE

This dish is an American cousin of Crêpes Suzette. It's easier than it seems, because it can be prepared in advance and reheated to serve.

1 cup all-purpose flour
1 tbsp oil
1 whole egg
1 egg yolk
1 cup milk (or more)
1lb cream cheese or low fat soft cheese
½ cup sugar
Grated rind of 1 orange
4 tbsps finely chopped pecans
Oil
½ cup orange juice mixed with 2 tsps cornstarch
4 oranges, peeled and segmented
4 tbsps orange liqueur

1. Sift the flour into a mixing bowl and make a well in the center.

2. Pour the 1 tbsp oil, whole egg and egg yolk into the center of the well and beat with a wooden spoon.

3. Gradually beat in the milk, incorporating the flour slowly. Set aside for 30 minutes.

4. Beat the cheese and sugar together with the orange rind until light and fluffy. Stir in the chopped pecans and set aside.

5. Heat a small crêpe pan or skillet over a medium heat and pour in a small amount of oil. Wipe the oil over the bottom of the pan with a paper towel to coat thinly.

6. Pour a small amount of batter (about 2 tbsps) into the hot pan and swirl the batter to coat the base evenly. Pour out the excess to re-use.

7. Cook until the bottom is a light golden brown and turn over. Cook the other side and stack up the crêpes on a plate. Repeat with remaining batter to make 12 small or 6 large crêpes.

8. Spread some of the filling on the speckled side of each crêpe and roll up or fold into triangles. Place in a warm oven, 325°, while preparing the sauce.

9. Pour orange juice and cornstarch mixture into a saucepan and bring to the boil over a low heat, stirring constantly. Boil until thickened and clear. Stir in the orange segments and liqueur. Spoon sauce over crêpes to serve.

Step 6 Pour batter into the hot pan and swirl to coat the base.

Step 7 When first side is brown, turn crêpe over, using a round-bladed knife.

Cook's Notes

Time
Preparation takes about 30 minutes and cooking takes about 45 minutes. Prepare ahead of time and reheat about 15 minutes in a slow oven. Reheat sauce separately.

Cook's Tip
Unfilled crêpes can be stacked between sheets of non-stick or wax paper, placed in plastic bags and frozen for up to 3 months. Thaw at room temperature, separate and use with a variety of sweet or savory fillings.

Serving Idea
Use canned, pitted cherries as an alternative sauce.

SERVES 8

BREAD PUDDING
WITH WHISKEY SAUCE

A childhood pudding made sophisticated by the addition
of a bourbon-laced sauce and stylish presentation.

½ loaf day-old French bread
2 cups milk
3 eggs
¾ cup raisins
1 tsp vanilla extract
Pinch ground ginger
Butter or margarine
½ cup butter
1 cup sugar
1 egg
4 tbsps bourbon
Nutmeg

1. Cut bread into small pieces and soak in the milk.

2. When the bread has softened, add the eggs, raisins, vanilla and ginger.

3. Grease 8 custard cups with butter or margarine and fill each with an equal amount of pudding mixture to within ½ inch of the top.

4. Place the cups in a roasting pan and pour in enough hot water to come halfway up the sides of the dishes. Bake in a preheated 350°F oven until risen and set – about 35-40 minutes.

5. When the puddings have cooked, combine the ½ cup butter and the sugar in the top of a double boiler and heat to dissolve butter.

6. Beat the egg and stir in a spoonful of the hot butter mixture. Add the egg to the double boiler and whisk over heat until thick. Allow to cool and add bourbon.

7. To serve, turn out puddings onto plates and surround with sauce. Sprinkle the tops with nutmeg.

Step 2 Soak bread in the milk before adding the eggs, raisins, vanilla and ginger.

Step 4 Bake the pudding until risen and set. The puddings are done when a skewer inserted in the middle comes out clean.

Step 7 Loosen puddings from the sides of the dishes and turn out carefully.

 *Cook's Notes*

 **Time**
Preparation takes about 40 minutes, giving bread time to absorb milk. Cooking takes about 35-40 minutes for the pudding and about 20 minutes for the sauce.

Cook's Tip
If desired, cook pudding in one large dish, increasing time to 1 hour. Spoon portions onto plates and pour over sauce.

 Serving Idea
Sauce may be prepared with brandy instead of whiskey.

SERVES 6

PERSIMMON PUDDING

A rich and satisfying pudding for autumn made
with this plump, bright orange fruit.
Spice it up with preserve or fresh ginger.

2-4 ripe persimmons or Sharon fruit (depending on size)
4 tbsps honey
Juice and rind of 1 small orange
1 egg
½ cup light cream
¾ cup all-purpose flour
½ tsp baking powder
½ baking soda
Pinch cinnamon and nutmeg
2 tbsps melted butter
1 small piece preserved ginger, finely chopped, or small piece freshly grated ginger
4 tbsps chopped walnuts or pecans
Whipped cream, orange segments and walnut or pecan halves to decorate

Orange sauce
1 cup orange juice
Sugar to taste
1 tbsp cornstarch
2 tbsps brandy or orange liqueur

1. Peel the persimmons or Sharon fruit by dropping them into boiling water for about 5 seconds. Remove to a bowl of cold water and leave to stand briefly before peeling.

2. Scoop out any seeds and purée the fruit until smooth. Add the honey, orange juice and rind, egg and cream, and process once or twice. Pour the mixture into a bowl.

3. Sift the flour, baking powder, baking soda and spices over the persimmon purée and gradually fold together. Stir in the melted butter, ginger and nuts and spoon into well buttered custard cups. Place in a roasting pan half full of water and bake until risen and set, about 45 minutes, in a preheated 350°F oven. Test by inserting a skewer into the middle. If the skewer comes out clean the puddings are set. Allow to cool slightly.

4. Combine all the sauce ingredients except the brandy and cook slowly, over a low heat, stirring continuously, until thickened and cleared. Stir in the brandy or orange liqueur.

5. When the puddings have cooled slightly, loosen them from the edge of the dish and turn out onto a plate. Spoon some of the sauce over each and decorate with whipped cream, orange segments and nuts.

Step 3 Gradually fold the dry ingredients into the persimmon purée using a large metal spoon or a rubber spatula.

Step 5 Spoon some of the sauce over each pudding to glaze it.

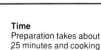 *Cook's Notes*

Time
Preparation takes about 25 minutes and cooking takes about 45 minutes.

Cook's Tip
To prevent a skin from forming on top of a dessert sauce, sprinkle lightly with sugar to cover the top completely. If using this method, adjust the quantity of sugar in the recipe.

Serving Idea
The pudding and sauce may be served warm or cold. If serving cold, cut the quantity of cornstarch down to 2 tsps, as the sauce will thicken on standing.

SERVES 4

BANANAS FOSTER

This rich concoction originated in a famous New Orleans
restaurant, but it's now a favorite on any Creole menu.

4 ripe bananas, peeled
½ cup butter
½ cup soft brown sugar, light or dark
Pinch ground cinnamon and nutmeg
4 tbsps orange juice
½ cup white or dark rum
Juice of ½ lemon
Whipped cream
Chopped pecans

Step 2 Combine butter, sugar and spices in a large skillet and heat gently to form a syrup.

Step 1 Cut the bananas carefully in half lengthwise.

Step 3 Baste the bananas frequently while cooking, but do not turn them.

1. Cut the bananas in half lengthwise and sprinkle with lemon juice on all sides.

2. Melt the butter in a large skillet and add the sugar, cinnamon, nutmeg and orange juice. Stir over gentle heat until the sugar dissolves into a syrup.

3. Add the banana halves and cook gently for about 3 minutes, basting the bananas often with syrup, but not turning them.

4. Once the bananas are heated through, warm the rum in a small saucepan or ladle over a low heat and ignite with a match. Pour the flaming rum over the bananas and shake the pan gently until the flames die down naturally. Place 2 banana halves on a serving plate and top with some of the whipped cream. Sprinkle with pecans and serve immediately.

Cook's Notes

Time
Preparation takes about 15 minutes and cooking takes about 5 minutes for the sugar and butter syrup and 3-4 minutes for the bananas.

Cook's Tip
Sprinkling the cut surfaces of the banana with lemon juice keeps them from turning brown and also offsets the sweetness of the sauce.

Serving Idea
The bananas may be served with vanilla ice cream instead of whipped cream, if desired.

HONEY AND APPLE TART

This delicious apple flan is wonderful served either hot or cold.

¾ cup whole-wheat flour
¾ cup all-purpose white flour
6 tbsps unsalted butter
1 egg yolk
3¾ tbsps cold water
1¼ cups unsweetened apple purée
1¼ tbsps honey
2 egg yolks
2½ tbsps ground almonds
3 large eating apples, quartered, cored and thinly sliced
Little pale soft brown sugar
3¾ tbsps clear honey, warmed to glaze

Step 4 Pinch the edges of the flan up, and prick the base with a fork.

1. Put the flours into a large bowl.

2. Cut the butter into the flour and mix together until the mixture resembles fine bread crumbs.

3. Beat the egg yolk and 2½ tbsps of the water together. Stir this into the dry ingredients, mixing to a firm soft dough and adding a little extra water if necessary.

4. Roll out the dough on a lightly floured surface and line a 9-inch loose-bottomed, fluted flan ring. Pinch up the edges well and prick the base to prevent it from rising during cooking.

5. Mix the apple purée with the honey, egg yolks and ground almonds, stirring well to blend thoroughly.

6. Spread this apple mixture evenly over the base of the pastry case.

7. Arrange the apple slices, overlapping slightly, in circles on the top of the apple and almond filling.

8. Sprinkle the top of the flan lightly with a little soft brown sugar, and bake in a preheated 375°F oven for 35-40 minutes, or until the apples are just beginning to go golden brown.

9. As soon as the flan is removed from the oven, carefully brush the top with the warmed honey glaze.

Step 7 Arrange the apple slices in circles overlapping each slice slightly, on the top of the apple and almond filling.

Cook's Notes

Time
Preparation takes 45 minutes, cooking takes about 40 minutes.

Cook's Tip
If the apples begin to brown before the end of cooking time, cover the tart with aluminum foil to prevent any further coloring.

Serving Idea
Serve with fresh whipped cream.

BROWN BREAD ICE CREAM

This unusual ice cream is easy to make and is an ideal
standby dessert to keep in the freezer.

2 egg yolks
⅓ cup superfine sugar
2 cups heavy or whipping cream
Few drops of vanilla extract
½ cup water
½ cup brown sugar
7 tbsps fresh brown bread crumbs
1¼ tsps ground cinnamon

1. Put the egg yolks and the superfine sugar into a bowl, and beat vigorously with an electric beater until thick, pale and creamy.

2. Pour in the heavy cream and continue beating until thick and creamy.

3. Beat in the vanilla extract, then pour the cream mixture into a freezer-proof container and freeze for 1 hour, or until beginning to set around the edges.

4. Break the ice cream away from the edges and beat with the electric beater until the ice crystals have broken. Return to the freezer and chill for a further hour. Repeat this procedure 2 more times, then freeze completely.

5. Put the water and the brown sugar into a small saucepan and heat over a low heat, stirring until the sugar has dissolved. Bring the mixture to the boil and boil rapidly until the sugar caramelizes.

6. Remove the caramel sugar from the heat and stir in the bread crumbs and the cinnamon.

7. Spread the caramel mixture onto a cookie sheet lined with oiled wax paper, and allow to set.

8. Break up the caramelized bread crumbs by placing them in plastic food bags and crushing with a rolling pin.

Step 1 Beat the eggs and superfine sugar together until they are pale, thick and creamy.

Step 7 When cooled, the caramelized bread crumbs should set completely hard.

9. Turn the frozen ice cream into a large bowl and break it up with a fork.

10. Allow the ice cream to soften slightly, then stir in the caramelized bread crumbs, mixing thoroughly to blend evenly.

11. Return the brown bread ice cream to the freezer tray and freeze completely.

12. Allow the mixture to soften for 10 minutes before serving in scoops.

Cook's Notes

Time
Preparation takes about 40 minutes, plus freezing time.

Cook's Tip
Be very careful when making the caramel sugar as it can burn very easily.

Serving Idea
Serve as an accompaniment to fruit salads.

PASSION FRUIT ICE CREAM

Fruit ice creams are actually more refreshing without added sugar, but if you must have added sweetness use liquid sweetener.

6 passion fruit
1¼ cups plain yogurt
2 egg yolks
Liquid sweetener to taste (optional)
1-2 passion fruit, halved and pulp scooped out for decoration

Step 4 Break up the partially frozen passion fruit ice cream using a fork, and mixing until a smooth slush is formed.

Step 1 Cut the six passion fruit in half and scoop all the center pulp into a bowl using a small spoon.

1. Halve the 6 passion fruit, and scoop out all the center pulp into a bowl.

2. Add the yogurt and egg yolks to the passion fruit pulp, and mix together well, adding liquid sweetener to taste, if desired.

3. Pour the passion fruit mixture into a shallow container, and freeze until partially set – approximately 1 hour.

Step 2 Beat together the yogurt, egg yolks and passion fruit pulp until they are well blended.

4. Break the ice crystals in the partially set passion fruit mixture using a fork, and mixing well until they form a smooth slush.

5. Return the ice cream to the freezer and freeze until completely firm.

6. To serve, remove the ice cream from the freezer for 20 minutes, then pile scoops of ice cream into stemmed glasses, and serve with passion fruit pulp poured over each portion.

Cook's Notes

Time
Preparation takes about 20 minutes, plus freezing time.

Cook's Tip
This ice cream goes extremely hard when frozen, so it is important to remember to remove it from the freezer 20 minutes before serving.

Serving Idea Serve with a sieved and sweetened raspberry purée.

STRAWBERRY YOGURT ICE

Ice cream is usually forbidden if someone's on a low calorie
diet, but when prepared with plain yogurt and fresh fruit, it can
provide a welcome treat.

1⅔ cups fresh strawberries
1⅓ cups plain yogurt
2½ tsps gelatin
2½ tbsps boiling water
1 egg white
Liquid sweetener to taste
Few fresh strawberries for decoration

Step 2 Blend the strawberries and yogurt together in a blender or food processor, until they are smooth.

1. Remove and discard the green stalks and leaves from the top of the strawberries. Roughly chop the fruit.

2. Place the strawberries into a blender, or food processor, along with the yogurt. Blend until smooth.

3. Sprinkle the gelatin over the boiling water in a small bowl. Stand the bowl into another, and pour in enough boiling water to come halfway up the sides of the dish.

4. Allow the gelatin to stand, without stirring, until it has dissolved and the liquid has cleared.

Step 5 Remove the strawberry mixture from the freezer when it is just beginning to set and has frozen around the edges.

5. Pour the strawberry mixture into a bowl, and stir in the dissolved gelatin, mixing well to blend evenly. Place the bowl into a deep freeze and chill until just icy around the edges.

6. Remove the bowl from the deep freeze and beat until the chilled mixture is smooth. Return the bowl to the deep freeze and freeze once again in the same way.

7. Remove the bowl from the deep freeze a second time, and beat with an electric mixer until smooth. Beat the egg white with a whisk until it forms soft peaks.

8. Fold the egg white into the partially set strawberry mixture, carefully lifting and cutting the mixture to keep it light.

9. Sweeten with liquid sweetener to taste, then pour the strawberry ice into a shallow sided ice cream dish, and return to the freezer to freeze until completely set.

10. Remove the ice cream 10 minutes before serving to soften slightly. Pile into serving dishes and decorate with a few extra strawberries.

Cook's Notes

Time
Preparation takes about 15 minutes, plus freezing time.

Cook's Tip
Use frozen or canned strawberries in place of the fresh strawberries, but drain all the juice away first.

Serving Idea
Serve with homemade cookies for those not on diets.

BLACK BOTTOM ICE CREAM PIE

Unbelievably simple, yet incredibly
delicious and impressive, this pie is a perfect
ending to a summer meal or a spicy one anytime.

8-10 Graham crackers
½ cup butter or margarine, melted
4oz shredded coconut
2oz semi-sweet chocolate, melted
3 cups coffee ice cream
Dark rum

Step 2 Press the crust mixture into the base of a loose-bottomed flan dish.

1. Crush crackers with a rolling pin or in a food processor. Mix with melted butter or margarine.

2. Press into an 8½-inch loose-bottomed flan dish. Chill thoroughly in the refrigerator.

3. Meanwhile, combine 4 tbsps of the coconut with the melted chocolate. When cooled but not solidified, add about a quarter of the coffee ice cream, mixing well.

4. Spread the mixture on the base of the crust and freeze until firm.

5. Soften the remaining ice cream with an electric mixer or food processor and spread over the chocolate-coconut layer. Re-freeze until firm.

6. Toast the remaining coconut in a moderate oven, 350°F, stirring frequently until pale golden brown. Allow to cool completely.

7. Remove the pie from the freezer and leave in the refrigerator 30 minutes before serving. Push up the base of the dish and place the pie on a serving plate. Sprinkle the top with toasted coconut. Cut into wedges and drizzle with rum before serving.

Step 4 Spread the chocolate, coconut and coffee cream mixture evenly over the bottom of the crust and freeze.

Step 5 Spread the remaining coffee ice cream carefully over the chocolate-coconut layer and re-freeze.

Cook's Notes

Time
Preparation takes about 25 minutes. The ice cream will take several hours to freeze.

Cook's Tip
The pie may be prepared well in advance and kept in the freezer for up to 3 months. Coconut may be sprinkled on top before freezing or just before serving.

Serving Idea
Serve as an unusual tea- or coffee-time treat.

FROZEN LIME AND BLUEBERRY CREAM

Blueberries grow wild in many parts of the United States and recipes to use them abound.

Juice and rind of 4 limes
Water
1 cup sugar
4oz blueberries
3 egg whites
1 cup heavy cream, whipped
Whipped cream, frosted blueberries (see decoration
  section), lime slices

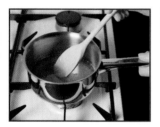

Step 3 Boil the lime juice, water and sugar rapidly once a clear syrup forms.

1. Measure the lime juice and make up to 6 tbsps with water if necessary.

2. Combine with the sugar in a heavy-based pan and bring to the boil slowly over a low heat to dissolve the sugar.

3. When the mixture forms a clear syrup, boil rapidly to 250°F on a sugar thermometer.

4. Meanwhile, combine the blueberries with about 4 tbsps water in a small saucepan. Bring to the boil over a low heat and then simmer, covered, until very soft. Purée, sieve to remove the seeds and skin, and set aside to cool.

5. Beat the egg whites with a whisk until stiff but not dry

and then pour on the hot sugar syrup in a steady stream, beating constantly. Add the lime rind and allow to cool.

6. When cold, fold in the whipped cream. Pour in the purée and marble through the mixture with a rubber spatula. Do not over-fold. Pour the mixture into a lightly-oiled mold or bowl and freeze overnight until firm. Leave 30 minutes in the refrigerator before serving, or dip the mold for about 10 seconds in hot water. Place a plate over the bottom of the mold, invert and shake to turn out. Decorate with extra whipped cream, frosted blueberries or lime slices.

Step 5 Pour the syrup gradually onto the beaten egg whites, beating constantly.

Step 6 Fold the cream and the fruit purée into the egg whites, marbling the purée through the mixture.

Cook's Notes

 Time
Preparation takes about
40 minutes. Freezing takes
overnight.

 Cook's Tip
Take care not to burn the
syrup

 Serving Idea
Serve with crisp cookies.

24

MANGO SORBET

This delicious cool sorbet can be used either as a dessert, or as a refresher between courses.

---

3 mangoes
Juice ½ lime
½ cup dry white wine
½ cup mineral water
1 egg white
Liquid sweetener to taste (optional)

---

1. Peel the mango and cut away the flesh from around the large center stone.

2. Put the mango flesh into a blender or food processor, and blend until smooth.

3. In a bowl, mix together the lime juice, wine and mineral water and add this to the mango purée.

4. Place the mango purée in a deep freeze and freeze until just beginning to set around the edges.

5. Break up the ice crystals in the mango mixture using a fork.

6. Beat the egg white with a whisk until it is stiff, then fold this carefully and thoroughly into the mango mixture. Sweeten with liquid sweetener to taste, if desired.

7. Return the mango mixture to the deep freeze, and freeze until completely set.

8. To serve, remove from the deep freeze 10 minutes before required, then spoon into individual serving dishes.

Step 2 Purée the mango flesh in a blender or food processor, until it is smooth.

Step 5 Break up the ice crystals which have formed in the mango mixture into small pieces using the back of a fork.

Cook's Notes

Time
Preparation takes about 15 minutes, plus freezing time.

Cook's Tip
This recipe works with other fruit, so experiment with the family's favorites.

Serving Idea
Serve with fresh fruit or decorate with fresh edible flowers.

MAKES 3 CUPS

GUAVA MINT SORBET

When a light dessert is called for, a sorbet can't be surpassed.
The exotic taste of guava works well with mint.

⅔ cup granulated sugar
1 cup water
4 ripe guavas
2 tbsps chopped fresh mint
1 lime
1 egg white
Fresh mint leaves to decorate

Step 4 Process the frozen mixture again and gradually work in the egg white.

Step 2 Combine the puréed guava, mint and cold syrup.

1. Combine the sugar and water in a heavy-based saucepan and bring slowly to the boil over a low heat to dissolve the sugar. When the mixture is a clear syrup, boil rapidly for 30 seconds. Allow to cool to room temperature and then chill in the refrigerator.

2. Cut the guavas in half and scoop out the pulp. Discard the peels and seeds and purée the fruit until smooth in a food processor. Add the mint and combine with the cold syrup. Add lime juice until the right balance of sweetness is reached.

Step 3 Freeze the mixture until slushy and then process to break up the ice crystals.

3. Pour the mixture into a shallow container and freeze until slushy. Process again to break up ice crystals and then freeze until firm.

4. Beat the egg white with a whisk until stiff but not dry. Process the sorbet again and when smooth, add the egg white. Mix once or twice and then freeze again until firm.

5. Remove from the freezer 15 minutes before serving and keep in the refrigerator.

6. Scoop out and decorate each serving with mint leaves.

Cook's Notes

 Time
Preparation takes about 2-3 hours, allowing the sorbet to freeze in between processing.

 Cook's Tip
The sorbet will keep in the freezer for up to 3 months in a well-sealed, rigid container.

Serving Idea
Guava Mint Sorbet makes a refreshing accompaniment to an exotic fruit salad, such as the Caribbean Fruit Salad.

FROZEN MERINGUE CREAM

he texture of this sorbet is similar to ice cream because
of the mixing during freezing.

4 cups light cream
⅓ cup sugar
1 whole vanilla bean
2 egg whites
4 tbsps brandy

Step 5 Beat the egg whites until stiff but not dry and fold into the cooled cream mixture before adding the brandy.

1. Combine the cream, sugar and vanilla bean in a deep, heavy-based saucepan.

2. Cook over a low heat for about 10 minutes, stirring frequently to dissolve the sugar. Do not allow the cream to boil.

3. Cover the pan and leave to infuse for about 15 minutes. Strain into a bowl to remove the vanilla bean and set aside to cool completely.

4. Beat the egg whites with a whisk until stiff but not dry.

5. Fold them into the cooled cream mixture. Add brandy and chill completely.

Step 6 Freeze the cream mixture in shallow containers or ice cube trays until slushy.

Step 7 Mix with an electric mixer or in a food processor until the mixture is smooth and then refreeze.

6. Pour into a shallow pan or ice cube tray and freeze until slushy.

7. Spoon the mixture into a food processor and work until smooth. Alternatively, use an electric mixer. Return the mixture to the freezer and freeze until nearly solid. Repeat the mixing procedure and then freeze in a rigid container until firm. Allow the container to stand at room temperature for about 10 minutes before serving.

Cook's Notes

Time
Preparation takes about 20 minutes. Allow at least 2 hours for the freezing and mixing procedure.

Cook's Tip
The freezing and mixing procedure eliminates large ice crystals from the sorbet. If desired, the sorbet may be processed again just before serving, but this will result in a very soft mixture.

Serving Idea
Serve with chocolate sauce, fruit sauce or caramelized fruit (see decoration section), cookies, or simply sprinkled with ground cinnamon or nutmeg.

CHESTNUT & ALMOND STUFFED PEACHES

A delicious combination of flavors.

4 large freestone peaches
1 cup dry white wine
2 tbsps brandy

Filling
2oz semi-sweet chocolate
2¾oz chestnut spread
1 egg yolk
1 tbsp peach liqueur or brandy
½ cup heavy cream
1 tbsp ground almonds
4 amaretti or ratafia biscuits
Cream (optional)

Step 4 Fold whipped cream into the chocolate chestnut mixture along with the almonds.

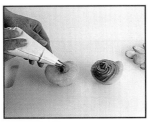

Step 6 Pipe the filling into the hollow in each peach half.

Step 1 Remove the peach stones using a small knife or swivel vegetable peeler.

1. Wash the peaches, peel them and cut them in half. Carefully remove the stones and place the peaches in a large bowl with the wine, brandy and enough water to cover them completely. Marinate for 1 hour.

2. Cut the chocolate into small pieces and melt in the top of a double boiler. Stir in the chestnut spread. Remove the chocolate from the heat and leave to cool for about 2 minutes, stirring frequently.

3. Beat in the egg yolk until well incorporated. Add the peach liqueur or brandy and stir well. Allow to cool.

4. Whip the cream and fold into the chocolate-chestnut mixture with the ground almonds. Allow to cool completely before using.

5. Remove the peaches from the marinade with a draining spoon and place them in serving dishes. Fill a pastry bag fitted with a large rosette tube with the chocolate-chestnut mixture.

6. Pipe out a large rosette of chocolate-chestnut mixture into the hollow of each peach half. Place a biscuit on top of each peach and serve chilled, with cream if desired.

Cook's Notes

 Time
Peaches take 1 hour to marinate, preparation takes about 40 minutes.

 Cook's Tip
Fresh peaches or nectarines must be placed in the wine and brandy mixture as soon as they are peeled or they will darken.

Serving Idea
Peach liqueur or brandy may be poured over each peach before filling, if desired.

SERVES 4-6

CHERRIES JUBILEE

This makes a special, elegant pudding, but an easy one, too.
The contrast of hot brandied cherries and cold ice cream or
whipped cream is sensational.

1½lb black cherries, fresh or canned
2-4 tbsps sugar
¾ cup brandy
Vanilla ice cream or whipped cream

Step 1 Pit cherries using a cherry pitter, vegetable peeler or small knife.

Step 1 Cook slowly with the sugar until the cherries soften and juices run.

Step 2 Heat brandy and ignite before pouring onto the fruit.

1. If using fresh cherries, wash them, remove the stems and pit, if desired, but leave the cherries whole. Combine them with 4 tbsps sugar in a saucepan and cook over a low heat until the cherries soften and the juices run. If using canned cherries, combine the juice with 2 tbsps sugar and heat through to dissolve the sugar. Pit the cherries, if desired, but leave them whole and add to the juice.

2. Pour the brandy into a separate saucepan or a large ladle. Heat the brandy over a medium heat and ignite with a match. Combine the brandy with the fruit and leave until the flames die down naturally.

3. Spoon the fruit over ice cream or on its own into serving dishes to be topped with whipped cream. Serve immediately.

Cook's Notes

Time
Preparation takes about 30 minutes if pitting the cherries, and cooking takes about 10 minutes.

Cook's Tip
If using fresh cherries, pit and cook in advance and set aside. Before adding the brandy, reheat the cherries until hot.

Serving Idea
Serve with the Brown Bread Ice Cream instead of the vanilla ice cream or whipped cream.

MANGO AND COCONUT WITH LIME SABAYON

The taste of mango with lime is sensational, especially when
served with the deliciously creamy sauce in this stylish dessert.

2 large, ripe mangoes, peeled and sliced
1 fresh coconut
2 egg yolks
4 tbsps sugar
Juice and grated rind of 2 limes
½ cup heavy cream, whipped

Step 3 Beat egg yolks and sugar until thick and light lemon in color.

1. Arrange thin slices of mango on plates.

2. Break coconut in half and then into smaller sections.
Shred the white pulp, taking care to avoid shredding the
brown skin. Use the coarse side of the grater and scatter
the coconut over the mango slices.

3. Place egg yolks and sugar in the top of a double boiler
or a large bowl. Beat with a whisk until very thick and lemon
colored.

4. Stir in the lime juice and place mixture over simmering
water over a low heat. Beat constantly while the mixture
gently cooks and becomes thick and creamy.

5. Remove from the heat and place in another bowl of iced
water to cool quickly. Beat the mixture while it cools.

6. Fold in the whipped cream and spoon onto the fruit.
Decorate with the lime rind.

Cook's Notes

Time
Preparation takes about
40 minutes and cooking
takes about 8 minutes.

Cook's Tip
It is important that the water
under the sabayon does not
boil. If it does, this can cause
curdling or cook the mixture too
quickly, resulting in a poor texture.

Serving Idea
Serve the sabayon with
other fruit such as papayas,
peaches, pineapple or berries.

SUMMER FRUITS PUDDING

A classic dessert, which makes good use of nutritious
fresh fruits.

1½lbs mixed, fresh soft fruit
½ cup unrefined granulated sugar
9-10 slices whole-wheat bread, thickly cut and with crusts
removed
Soft fruit, to decorate

---

1. Put all the fruit into a saucepan with the sugar and heat
over a low heat, until the sugar has dissolved, but the fruit is
not completely cooked. Shake the pan while heating, so
that the fruit will stay as whole as possible.

2. Remove the pan from the heat and leave the fruit to
cool.

3. Line the base and sides of a 3-cup pudding basin with
6 or 7 slices of the bread, trying not to leave any gaps between each slice.

4. Put the fruit mixture into the center of the pudding, and
cover the top completely with the remaining bread slices.

Step 3 Line the
base and sides of a
3 cup pudding basin
with 6 or 7 slices of
the bread, making
sure that there are
no gaps between
the slices.

5. Press the top bread slices down firmly, and place a
saucer, or small plate, on top of the pudding. Weigh the
plate down with a heavy weight.

6. Chill the pudding in the refrigerator overnight. Turn the
pudding out of the bowl carefully, and decorate with fresh
soft fruit according to choice.

Cook's Notes

Time
Preparation takes about
10-15 minutes, plus
overnight chilling time.

Cook's Tip
If you do not have a heavy
weight handy, a bag of
sugar, or flour, will do equally well.

Serving Idea
Serve with a spoonful of
fromage frais or cream.

SUNBURST FIGS

Fresh figs can make a most attractive dessert and have the
added benefit of being very low in calories.

---

4 fresh figs
⅔ cup redcurrants in small bunches
6 oranges
1¼ tsps orange flower water

Step 3 Carefully press open the quarters of each fig to make an attractive flower shape.

Step 2 Cut the figs into quarters lengthwise with a sharp knife, taking great care not to sever the fruit completely through the base.

Step 7 Cut the orange segments away from the peeled fruit with a sharp knife, slicing carefully between the flesh and the thin membranes inside each segment.

1. Trim the stalks away from the top of the figs, but do not peel them.

2. Cut the figs into quarters lengthwise, taking care not to sever them completely at the base.

3. Press the fig quarters open gently with your fingers, to make a flower shape. Place each fig carefully on a serving plate.

4. Arrange the small bunches of reducrrants carefully on the center of each fig.

5. Cut 2 of the oranges in half, and squeeze out the juice. Mix this juice with the orange flower water in a small jug.

6. Carefully cut away the peel and white pith from the re-maining 4 oranges.

7. Using a sharp knife, cut the segments of orange away from the inside of the thin membranes, keeping each piece intact as a crescent shape.

8. Arrange the orange segments in between the petals of the fig flower on the serving plate.

9. Spoon equal amounts of the orange sauce over each fig, and chill thoroughly before serving.

Cook's Notes

Time
Preparation takes about 15 minutes, plus chilling time.

Cook's Tip
Use ruby grapefruit segments and blackcurrants in place of the oranges and redcurrants for a refreshing change.

Serving Idea
Frost the currants (see decoration section) before placing them on the figs, to give an attractive finish to this dessert.

BLACKBERRY FLUFF

Fresh blackberries have a delicious flavor, especially the wild
ones picked from hedgerows.

1lb fresh blackberries
1⅓ cups plain yogurt
2 egg whites
Liquid sweetener to taste
Pieces of angelica and whole blackberries to decorate

---

1. Wash the blackberries thoroughly and place them in a saucepan with no extra water, other than that which is left on their surfaces after washing. Cover the pan with a tight fitting lid, and cook over a low heat for 5-10 minutes, stirring occasionally until the fruit has softened. Cool slightly.

2. Press the cooked blackberries through a nylon sieve, using the back of a spoon to press out the juice and pulp. Discard the pips and reserve the purée.

3. Put the yogurt into a large bowl and beat in the blackberry purée until it is smooth.

4. Beat the egg whites with a whisk until they form very stiff peaks.

5. Fold these into the blackberry purée, trying not to over mix the ingredients, so as to create an attractive marbled effect.

6. Sweeten with the liquid sweetener to taste, then pile into serving dishes and decorate with the whole blackberries and angelica pieces. Chill before serving.

Step 4 Beat the egg whites until they form very stiff peaks.

Step 2 Press the cooked blackberries through a sieve, using the back of a wooden spoon to push through the juice and pulp, leaving the pips in the sieve.

Step 5 Lightly fold the egg whites into the blackberry mixture, to create an attractive marbled effect.

Cook's Notes

Time
Preparation takes about 20 minutes. Cooking time takes approximately 10 minutes, plus chilling time.

Cook's Tip
Use other soft fruits in season, e.g. raspberries or strawberries.

Serving Idea
This recipe can also be partially frozen to create a cooling summer dessert.

SPICED ORANGES WITH HONEY AND MINT

An unusual combination of flavors blend to create this light and very refreshing dessert.

1¼ cups clear honey
1½ cups water
2 large sprigs of fresh mint
12 whole cloves
4 large oranges
4 small sprigs of mint, to decorate

1. Put the honey and the water into a heavy-based saucepan over a low heat. Add the mint and cloves, and slowly bring to the boil.

2. Stir the mixture to dissolve the honey, increase the heat and boil rapidly for 5 minutes, or until the liquid is very syrupy.

3. Cool the mixture completely, then strain the syrup through a nylon sieve into a jug or bowl to remove the sprigs of mint and cloves.

4. Using a potato peeler, carefully pare the rind very thinly from one orange.

5. Cut the pared orange rind into very fine shreds with a sharp knife.

6. Put the shreds of orange peel into a small bowl and cover with boiling water. Allow to stand until cold then drain completely, reserving only the strips of peel.

7. Stir the strips of peel into the honey syrup and chill well.

8. Peel the oranges completely, removing all the skin and especially the white pith.

Step 3 Strain the syrup through a nylon sieve into a jug or bowl to remove the sprigs of mint and cloves.

Step 4 Carefully pare the rind from one of the oranges, using a potato peeler and making sure that no white pith comes away with the rind.

9. Slice the oranges into thin rounds using a sharp knife. Arrange the orange rounds onto four individual serving plates.

10. Pour the chilled syrup over the oranges on the plates and decorate with the small sprigs of mint just before serving.

Cook's Notes

Time
Preparation takes 20 minutes, cooking takes about 5 minutes.

Cook's Tip
It is important that all the white pith is removed from the oranges, otherwise this will give a bitter flavor to the dessert.

Serving Idea
Use ruby grapefruits in place of the oranges in this recipe. Allow half a grapefruit per person, and cut it into segments rather than slices to serve.

CARIBBEAN FRUIT SALAD

This fruit salad is made from a refreshing mixture of tropical fruits, all of which are now readily available in most supermarkets.

½ cantaloupe or honeydew melon, seeds removed
½ small pineapple
¼lb fresh strawberries
1 mango
½lb watermelon
¼ guava
2 oranges
½ cup superfine sugar
⅔ cup white wine
Grated rind and juice of 1 lemon

1. Using a melon baller or teaspoon, scoop out rounds of flesh from the cantaloup or honeydew melon.

2. Cut the piece of pineapple in half lengthwise and carefully peel away the outer skin.

3. Remove any eyes left in the outside edge of the pineapple using a potato peeler.

4. Cut away the core from the pineapple with a serrated knife and slice the flesh thinly. Put the slices of pineapple into a large bowl along with the melon rounds.

5. Hull the strawberries and halve them. Add them to the bowl with the pineapple and melon.

6. Peel the mango, and carefully cut the flesh away from the long stone in the center of the fruit. Slice the flesh lengthwise, and stir it into the bowl of fruit.

7. Peel the watermelon and guava, then cube the flesh. Stir these into the bowl of fruit.

8. Remove the rind from the oranges using a serrated knife. Take care to remove all the white pith, or this will give a bitter flavor to the fruit salad.

9. Cut the orange into segments, carefully removing the inner membrane from the segments as you slice.

10. Put the sugar, wine, lemon juice and rind into a small saucepan and warm through over a low heat, stirring all the time until the sugar has dissolved. Do not boil, but set aside to cool.

11. Put the syrup into the bowl along with the fruit and mix thoroughly. Chill the fruit salad completely before serving.

Step 3 Remove any eyes which remain in the pineapple flesh with the pointed end of a potato peeler.

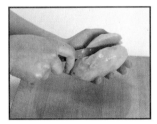

Step 6 Carefully cut the flesh away from the long inner stone of the mango, before slicing it lengthwise.

Cook's Notes

Time
Preparation takes 45 minutes, cooking takes about 3 minutes.

Cook's Tip
Do not boil the syrup otherwise the flavor of the wine will be reduced.

Serving Idea
Serve in a melon basket (see decoration section) for maximum visual appeal.

PEARS IN ZINFANDEL

Zinfandel has a spicy taste that complements pears
beautifully. Add a garnish of crisp almonds for a Californian
version of a French classic.

3 cups Zinfandel or other dry red wine
1 cup sugar
1 cinnamon stick
1 strip lemon peel
6 Bosc pears, even sized
4 tbsps slivered almonds
1 tbsp cornstarch mixed with 3 tbsps water
Mint leaves to decorate

1. Pour the wine into a deep saucepan that will hold the pears standing upright.

2. Add sugar, cinnamon and lemon peel, and bring to a boil over a low heat to dissolve the sugar. Stir constantly.

3. Peel pears, remove "eye" on the bottom, but leave on the stems.

4. Stand the pears close together in the wine, so that they remain standing. Cover the pan and poach gently over low heat for about 25-35 minutes, or until tender. If the wine does not cover the pears completely, baste the tops frequently as they cook.

5. Meanwhile, toast almonds on a baking sheet in a moderate oven, 350°F, for about 8-10 minutes, stirring them occasionally for even browning. Remove and allow to cool.

6. When pears are cooked, remove from the liquid to a serving dish. Boil the liquid over a high heat to reduce it by about half. If it is still too thin to coat the pears, thicken it with 1 tbsp cornstarch dissolved in 3 tbsps water.

7. Pour syrup over the pears and sprinkle with almonds. Serve warm or refrigerate until lightly chilled. Decorate pears with mint leaves at the stems just before serving.

Step 3 Peel pears and remove the "eye" on the base of each.

Step 4 Stand the pears upright in the saucepan.

Step 7 The syrup should be thick enough to coat the pears lightly.

 *Cook's Notes*

 **Time**
Preparation takes about 25 minutes and cooking takes about 50 minutes.

Cook's Tip
Use white wine to poach the pears, and flavor with cinnamon or a vanilla bean to ring the changes.

 Serving Idea
Serve with whipped cream, ice cream or custard for a richer dessert.

CARROT CAKE

Carrots give a cake a delicious sweet flavor, as well as lots of vitamins and minerals. What better excuse do you need to indulge in this delicious tea-time treat.

¾ cup butter
¾ cup Barbados sugar
2 eggs, well beaten
2 cups all-purpose whole-wheat flour
2 tsps baking soda
¾ tsp baking powder
½ tsp ground cinnamon
½ tsp ground nutmeg
¾ tsp salt
½lb peeled carrots, grated
⅔ cup raisins
½ cup finely chopped walnuts
½ tsp cardamom seeds, crushed
Confectioners' sugar, for dredging

3. Put the remaining flour into a large bowl along with the bicarbonate of soda, baking powder, cinnamon, nutmeg and salt. Mix together well.

4. Carefully fold the flour into the butter and egg mixture, mixing well to ensure that it is blended evenly.

5. Add the carrots, raisins, nuts and cardamom seeds, beating the mixture well to blend evenly.

6. Lightly grease a 10-inch loaf pan and line the base with a piece of silicone paper.

7. Pour the cake mixture into the loaf pan, and bake in a preheated 350°F oven, for 45-50 minutes or until a fine metal skewer comes out clean when inserted into the center of the cake.

8. Cool the cake in its pan for 15 minutes before turning out onto a wire rack to cool completely.

9. Dredge the cake with confectioners' sugar just before serving.

Step 2 Beat the eggs gradually into the butter and sugar, adding a little flour with each addition to prevent the mixture from curdling.

Step 5 Stir the carrots, fruit and nuts into the cake mixture, mixing well to blend evenly.

1. Beat the butter and sugar together until they are light and fluffy.

2. Add the eggs a little at a time, beating well and adding a teaspoonful of the flour with each addition, to prevent the mixture from curdling.

Cook's Notes

 Time
Preparation takes 30 minutes, cooking takes 45-50 minutes.

 Cook's Tip
If the egg and butter mixture should curdle, add a little more flour and beat very hard with an electric whisk until the curdling disappears.

 Serving Idea
Spread with lemon and cream cheese frosting in place of the confectioners' sugar.

TOASTED ALMOND CAKE

This mouthwatering cake makes a deliciously different
dessert.

⅔ cup butter, softened
½ cup superfine sugar
2 eggs, lightly beaten
1½ cups whole-wheat self-rising flour
¾ tsp vanilla extract
2½ tbsps orange juice
⅓ cup Barbados sugar
¼ cup melted, unsalted butter
1¼ tbsps milk
½ cup slivered almonds
½ cup confectioners' sugar
2½ tbsps cornstarch
3 egg yolks
½ cup milk
⅓ cup heavy cream, whipped
½ tsp almond extract

---

1. Beat the butter and superfine sugar until it is light and fluffy.

2. Beat in the eggs one at a time, adding a teaspoonful of the flour with each addition to prevent the mixture from curdling.

3. Fold in all the remaining flour, along with the vanilla extract and the orange juice.

4. Lightly grease an 8-inch cake pan, and line the base with a piece of silicone paper.

5. Spoon the cake mixture into the pan and smooth the top evenly with a round-bladed knife.

6. Put the brown sugar into a small saucepan, along with the melted butter, the 1¼ tbsps milk and the slivered almonds. Stir over a low heat until the sugar has completely dissolved.

7. Sprinkle about 1¼ tbsps of additional flour over the top of the cake mixture in the pan, then pour over the melted sugar, butter and almond mixture. Spread it evenly, but try not to disturb the cake mixture too much.

8. Bake the cake in a preheated 375°F oven for 20-30 minutes, or until the cake is well risen and the topping has caramelized golden brown.

9. Put the confectioners' sugar, cornstarch and egg yolks into a bowl and, using an electric beater, beat until they are light and fluffy.

10. Pour on the milk, beating well between additions. Strain this egg yolk mixture through a sieve into a heavy-based saucepan.

11. Cook the egg yolk and milk mixture over a low heat until it begins to thicken, and will thickly coat the back of a wooden spoon. Stir the mixture frequently during the cooking time to prevent it from burning or curdling.

12. Remove from the heat and cool.

13. When the custard is completely cool, lightly fold in the cream and the almond extract.

14. When the cake has cooled, carefully cut in half horizontally with a sharp knife. Sandwich the two halves back together using the almond custard as a filling.

15. Chill thoroughly before serving.

Cook's Notes

 Time
Preparation takes
40 minutes. Cooking takes
about 30 minutes, plus 10 minutes for
the filling.

 Cook's Tip
Do not allow the almond
topping to become too hot.
Heat it just long enough to dissolve
the sugar. If it does overheat, allow it
to cool before pouring onto the
uncooked cake mixture.

 Serving Idea
Serve as a tea- or coffee-
time treat.

CINNAMON BUTTER CREAM CAKE

This sumptuous cake has the added advantage of requiring no cooking.

1⅓ cup granulated sugar
7½ tbsps water
¾ tsp ground cinnamon
8 egg yolks
2 cups unsalted butter, softened
48 ladyfingers
10 tbsps brandy
1 cup toasted almonds, roughly chopped
1 cup unsweetened chocolate, coarsely grated

Step 9 Line the cake pan with trimmed ladyfingers spread with approximately half of the buttercream.

1. Put the sugar, water and cinnamon in a small heavy-based saucepan and bring to the boil over a medium heat, stirring constantly until the sugar dissolves.

2. Allow the sugar syrup to boil briskly without stirring, until it begins to thicken, but has not browned. This temperature should be 236° on a sugar thermometer; or when the sugar mixture will form a small ball when dropped into a bowl of cold water.

3. Beat the egg yolks in a large bowl with an electric mixer, until they are pale and thick.

4. Pour the sugar syrup quickly, in a thin steady stream, into the beaten egg yolks, beating constantly with the electric mixer.

5. Continue beating in this way until the mixture is thick, smooth and creamy. Allow to cool at room temperature.

6. Still using the electric mixer, beat the softened butter, a spoonful at a time, into the egg and sugar mixture. Beat well to ensure that it is evenly distributed. Chill the mixture until it reaches spreading consistency.

7. Line an 8-inch square cake pan with greased foil or silicone paper.

8. Cut the ladyfingers into neat pieces to enable you to use them to line the cake pan.

9. Divide the butter cream in half and spread a little of the buttercream lightly on one side of each biscuit and place them, cream side down, into the pan.

10. Cut any small pieces of biscuits to fill any corners, if necessary.

11. Continue spreading the buttercream on the ladyfingers and lining the cake pan in this way, alternating the direction of the fingers between the layers.

12. Once half the ladyfingers have been used in this way, sprinkle them with half the brandy. Continue layering and sprinkle with the remaining brandy. Chill in the refrigerator overnight.

13. Remove the cake from the pan and peel off the paper or foil. Slide the cake onto a flat surface and coat with the remaining half of the buttercream.

14. Press the chopped almonds onto the sides of the cake and decorate the top with the grated chocolate. Serve immediately, or chill in the refrigerator until required.

Cook's Notes

 Time
Preparation takes about 45 minutes, plus overnight chilling.

 Cook's Tip
This cake freezes well.

 Serving Idea
This delicious cake is perfect dinner-party fare.

AMERICAN RICE CAKES

These small rice cakes are crisp outside, soft and light inside.
They are delicious served hot with coffee or tea.

1 cup all purpose flour
1 tsp baking powder
Pinch salt
½ cup sugar
2 eggs, separated
6 tbsps milk
1½-2 cups long-grain rice, cooked
Grated rind of 1 lemon
4 tbsps raisins
Powdered sugar

Step 3 Beat the egg whites until stiff peaks form.

1. Sift the flour, baking powder and salt into a mixing bowl and stir in the sugar.

2. Beat the yolks with the milk and add gradually to the dry ingredients, stirring constantly, to make a thick batter. Stir in enough cooked rice to the mixture until it forms a stiff batter.

3. Beat the egg whites with a whisk until stiff but not dry, and fold into the batter along with the lemon rind and raisins.

4. Lightly oil the base of a heavy skillet and place over a medium heat. When the pan is hot, drop in about 1 tbsp of batter and if necessary, spread into a small circle with the back of a spoon.

5. Cook until brown on one side and bubbles form on the top surface. Turn over and cook the other side. Cook 4-6 at a time.

6. Repeat until all the batter is used, keeping the cakes warm. Sprinkle with powdered sugar and serve.

Step 3 Mix a spoonful of whites into the rice mixture to lighten it. Fold in the remaining whites using a large spoon.

Step 4 Drop the mixture by spoonfuls into a hot frying pan. Cook until brown on both sides.

Cook's Notes

Time
Preparation takes about 40 minutes and cooking takes about 40-45 minutes.

Cook's Tip
To drain rice thoroughly, place in a colander and make several drainage holes with the handle of a wooden spoon.

Serving Idea
Squeeze lemon juice over hot rice cakes, or spoon on jam. Cakes can also be served cold.

MARDI GRAS CAKES

A different version of the King's cake, made to celebrate this
famous Lenten carnival in New Orleans. The three colors
symbolize justice, power and faith.

1 package dried active yeast
6 tbsps lukewarm water
2 tsps sugar
2 cups all-purpose flour
4 tbsps additional sugar
Pinch salt
1 tsp ground ginger
Grated rind of 1 lemon
2 eggs
6 tbsps lukewarm milk
4 tbsps butter or margarine, cut in small pieces
4oz golden raisins, currants and chopped, candied fruit

Icing
¾ cup granulated sugar
Purple, yellow and green food colorings
2 cups powdered sugar
Juice 1 lemon
Hot water

1. Sprinkle the yeast on top of the lukewarm water and stir in the sugar. Set in a warm place to prove for 15 minutes, or until bubbly.

2. Sift the flour, sugar, salt and ginger into a large bowl and add the lemon rind. Make a well in the center of the ingredients and pour in the yeast. Add the eggs and milk.

3. Beat well, drawing the flour in from the outside edge, and gradually add the butter, a few pieces at a time.

4. Turn the dough out onto a well-floured surface and knead until smooth and elastic, about 10 minutes. Place the dough in a large, lightly-oiled bowl and cover with oiled plastic wrap.

5. Leave to rise in a warm place for 1-1½ hours, or until doubled in bulk.

6. Knock the dough back and knead in the fruit to distribute it evenly.

7. Oil a 12-space muffin pan. Divide the dough in 12 and knead each piece into a smooth ball. Place a ball in each space in the pan and cover lightly. Leave in a warm place for 20-30 minutes to rise a second time. Bake at 375°F for about 20-25 minutes, or until golden brown. Allow to cool slightly and loosen the cakes. Cool completely before removing from the pan.

8. Place an equal portion of sugar in each of three jars and add a drop of different food coloring to each. Shake the jars to color the sugar.

9. Sift the powdered sugar and mix with the lemon juice. Add enough hot water to make an icing that pours easily but still clings to the back of a spoon. Spoon some icing over each cake and sprinkle the cakes with the different colored sugars before the icing sets.

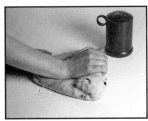

Step 6 When the dough has risen the first time, knock back and knead in the fruit to distribute it evenly.

Cook's Notes

Time
Preparation takes about 40 minutes. This does not include rising times for the yeast dough. Cooking takes about 20-25 minutes.

Cook's Tip
The cakes may be prepared the day before and kept in airtight containers. Ice and decorate with sugar on the day of serving.

Serving Idea
Mardi Gras cakes are a hit with children anytime.

SYRUP CAKE

Rather like gingerbread, but with a spicy taste of cinnamon,
nutmeg and cloves instead, this cake can be served cool with
coffee or tea or warm with cream.

l cup vegetable shortening
1 cup molasses
3 eggs, beaten
3 cups all-purpose flour
Pinch salt
1 tbsp baking powder
1 tsp cinnamon
¼ tsp ground nutmeg
Pinch ground cloves
4 tbsps chopped pecans
4 tbsps raisins

3. Stir in the nuts and raisins and pour the mixture into a lightly greased 9 × 13-inch baking pan.

4. Bake for about 45 minutes in a preheated 375° oven.

5. To test for doneness, insert a skewer into the center of the cake. If it comes out clean, the cake is done. Allow to cool and cut into squares to serve.

Step 2 Sift in the dry ingredients and stir well.

Step 1 Cream the shortening until light and fluffy. Beat in the molasses with an electric mixer.

Step 5 Insert a skewer into the center of the cake. If it comes out clean the cake is done.

1. Cream the shortening until light and fluffy. Add the molasses and beat with an electric mixer. Add the eggs one at a time, beating well between each addition.

2. Sift the flour together with a pinch of salt and baking powder. Combine with the molasses mixture and add the spices.

Cook's Notes

Time
Preparation takes about 20 minutes and cooking takes about 45 minutes.

Cook's Tip
Lightly oil the inside of the measuring cup when measuring syrups like molasses. The syrup will not stick to the cup but will pour right out.

Serving Idea
This cake is also a good store cupboard standby for lunch boxes.

CHOCOLATE SPICE CAKE

What a difference! The addition of spices sets this cake apart
from ordinary chocolate cakes.

5 eggs, separated
¾ cup superfine sugar
3oz bitter chocolate, melted
¾ cup all-purpose flour
½ tsp ground nutmeg
½ tsp ground cinnamon
½ tsp ground cloves

Topping
1 tbsp confectioners' sugar
1 tsp ground cinnamon

1. Grease and line an 8-inch spring-form cake pan with wax paper.

2. Brush the paper with melted butter and dust with a little extra flour.

3. Put the egg yolks and sugar into a mixing bowl and beat them hard, until the mixture is thick and creamy.

4. Stir in the melted chocolate and sift in the flour and spices. Fold in.

5. Beat the egg whites with a whisk until they are stiff and form soft peaks. Fold carefully into the chocolate mixture.

6. Pour the cake mixture into the prepared pan and bake in a preheated oven, 350°F, for 40-45 minutes, or until a skewer inserted into the middle of the cake comes out clean.

7. Leave the cake to cool in the tin for 10 minutes, then turn out onto a wire rack and leave to cool completely.

8. Mix together the confectioners' sugar and cinnamon. Sift this over the top of the cake before serving.

Step 1 Line the pan with wax paper. Fit a circle of paper in the bottom and carefully lay a strip of paper around the sides, clipping the bottom edge, so that it sits in neatly. Lay another paper circle over the clipped edge on the base.

Step 3 Beat the egg yolks and sugar together vigorously, until they are as thick and creamy as softly whipped heavy cream.

Step 8 Mix together the confectioners' sugar and cinnamon and sift this over the cake.

Cook's Notes

Time
Preparation takes 30 minutes, and cooking takes about 40-45 minutes.

Cook's Tip
Beating the egg yolks and sugar to the required consistency is easier if done over a pan of gently simmering water.

Serving Idea
Serve with whipped cream as a special treat.

MOIST FRUIT CAKE

Dark and moist, this delicious cake is full of fiber and
wholesome ingredients.

1 cup margarine
¾ cup unrefined soft brown sugar
1 cup Guinness or stout
1 cup raisins
1 cup currants
1 cup golden raisins
½ cup chopped mixed peel
1¼lb whole-wheat all-purpose flour
1 tsp mixed spice
1 tsp nutmeg
½ tsp bicarbonate of soda
3 eggs, beaten

1. Grease and line a 9-inch cake pan with wax or silicone paper.

2. Put the margarine, the sugar and the Guinness into a large saucepan over a low heat and bring the ingredients slowly to the boil, stirring all the time, until the sugar and the margarine have melted.

3. Stir the dried fruit and peel into the Guinness mixture, and bring all the ingredients back to the boil. Simmer for 5 minutes. Remove from the heat and leave, until the mixture is quite cold.

4. Put the flour, spices and bicarbonate of soda into a large mixing bowl.

5. Beat the cooled fruit mixture and the eggs into the flour, mixing well with a wooden spoon, to ensure that the flour is thoroughly incorporated and there are no lumps.

6. Pour the cake mixture into the prepared pan, and bake in the center of a preheated oven, 325°F, for 2 hours.

7. Cool the cake in the pan, before turning it out.

Step 1 Line the base and the sides of the greased cake pan with wax or silicone paper, making sure that it fits well into the corners and over the base of the pan.

Step 3 Simmer the dried fruit and peel in the sugar and Guinness mixture for 5 minutes, stirring occasionally.

Cook's Notes

Time
Preparation takes about 20 minutes, plus cooling time, and cooking takes about 2 hours.

Cook's Tip
To test whether the cake is cooked, push a metal skewer or darning needle into the center of the cake. If it is clean when pulled out, the cake is done.

Serving Idea
This cake is ideal to be used as a Christmas or rich birthday cake and can be decorated to suit the occasion with almond paste and frosting.

SPICED CRANBERRY NUT BREAD

Sassamanesh was the colorful Native American name for this
equally colorful berry. Here, it brightens up a quickly prepared bread.

2 cups all-purpose flour
1 tsp baking powder
1 cup sugar
1 tsp baking soda
Pinch salt
¼ tsp ground nutmeg
¼ tsp ground ginger
½ cup orange juice
2 tbsps butter or margarine, melted
4 tbsps water
1 egg
1 cup fresh cranberries, roughly chopped
1 cup hazelnuts, roughly chopped
Confectioners' sugar (optional)

Step 1 Sift the dry ingredients into a bowl and make a well in the center.

1. Sift the dry ingredients into a large mixing bowl. Make a well in the center of the dry ingredients and pour in the orange juice, melted butter or margarine, water and egg. Using a wooden spoon, beat the liquid mixture, gradually drawing in the flour from the outside edge.

2. Add the cranberries and nuts and stir to mix completely.

3. Lightly grease a loaf pan about 9 × 5 inches. Press a strip of wax paper onto the base and up the sides. Lightly grease the paper and flour the whole inside of the pan. Spoon or pour in the bread mixture and bake in a preheated 325°F oven for about 1 hour, or until a skewer inserted into the center of the loaf comes out clean.

4. Remove from the pan, carefully peel off the paper and cool on a wire rack. Lightly dust with confectioners' sugar, if desired, and cut into slices to serve.

Step 1 Pour the liquid ingredients into the well and, using a wooden spoon, stir to gradually incorporate the flour from the outside edge.

Step 2 Mix in the cranberries and the nuts.

Cook's Notes

Time
Preparation takes about 25 minutes and cooking takes about 1 hour.

Cook's Tip
Be sure to bake the bread mixture as soon as possible after the baking powder has been added or the bread will not rise the way it should.

Serving Idea
Serve warm with butter or cream cheese with tea or coffee. May also be served cold.

GRIDDLE SCONES

The whole fun of these cakes is that they can be eaten directly
from the pan in which they are cooked. So gather family and
friends around you for a traditional tea-time treat.

1 cup self-rising flour
Pinch salt
3 tbsps butter or margarine
⅔ cup currants
¾ tsp ground nutmeg
1 egg
⅓ cup milk
Preserves

Step 4 Using a
wooden spoon, mix
the egg and milk
mixture into the
flour, stirring from
the center of the
bowl and drawing
the flour in from the
sides to form a
smooth, thick batter.

Step 1 Rub the
butter into the flour
with your fingertips,
until the mixture
resembles fine
breadcrumbs.

Step 6 Fry
tablespoonfuls of
the batter in a hot
pan until the
undersides have
browned lightly and
the tops are just set.

1. Mix the flour and salt together, and rub in the butter until
the mixture resembles fine bread crumbs.

2. Stir in the currants and the nutmeg, then push the mixture gently to the sides of the bowl to form a well in the
center.

3. Beat together the egg and the milk, and pour into the
well in the center of the flour.

4. Using a wooden spoon, mix the egg and milk mixture
into the flour, stirring from the center of the bowl and drawing the flour in from the sides to form a smooth, thick batter.

5. Heat a heavy-based skillet over a medium heat, and
grease with a little butter or oil.

6. Drop tablespoonfuls of the batter into the hot pan, and
cook for 2-3 minutes, or until the bases are set and have
turned golden brown.

7. Turn the scones over and cook on the other side in the
same way.

8. Serve from the pan with preserves.

Cook's Notes

 Time
Preparation takes
15 minutes, cooking takes
about 4-6 minutes per batch of
scones.

 Cook's Tip
If the batter is too thick, add
a little extra milk until it
reaches a soft dropping consistency.

Serving Idea
Griddle scones make a
great treat for breakfast.

MAKES ABOUT 36

BROWN SUGAR COOKIES

This rather thick dough bakes to a crisp golden brown cookie,
perfect as an accompaniment to ice cream or fruit salad.

1¼ cups packed light brown sugar
3 tbsps light corn syrup
4 tbsps water
1 egg
2⅓ cups all-purpose flour
1 tbsp ground ginger
1 tbsp bicarbonate of soda
Pinch salt
1 cup finely chopped pecans

3. Lightly oil three baking sheets and place the mixture in spoonfuls about 2 inches apart.

4. Bake in a preheated 375°F oven until lightly browned around the edges, about 10-12 minutes. Leave on the baking sheet for 1-2 minutes before removing with a round-bladed knife to a wire rack to cool completely.

Step 3 Use a spoon to place the batter in spoonfuls about 2 inches apart onto a greased baking sheet.

Step 1 Combine the sugar, syrup, water and egg with an electric mixer until light.

Step 4 Bake until browned around the edges. Cool slightly and remove with a round-bladed knife.

1. Mix the brown sugar, syrup, water and egg together in a large bowl. Beat with an electric mixer until light.

2. Sift flour with the ginger, baking soda and salt into the brown sugar mixture and add the pecans. Stir by hand until thoroughly mixed.

Cook's Notes

 Time
Preparation takes about 20 minutes and cooking takes about 10-12 minutes per batch.

Cook's Tip
The dough will keep in the refrigerator for several days. Allow to stand at room temperature for at least 15 minutes before using.

 Serving Idea
Sandwich together with a cream filling and serve with coffee.

PECAN TASSIES

Like miniature pecan pies, these small pastries are popular
throughout the Southern states, especially at Christmas.

Pastry
½ cup butter or margarine
6 tbsps cream cheese
1 cup all-purpose flour

Filling
¾ cup chopped pecans
1 egg
¾ cup packed light brown sugar
1 tbsp softened butter
1 tsp vanilla extract
Powdered sugar

Step 2 Roll the dough into 1-inch balls and chill until firm.

1. Beat the butter or margarine and cheese together to soften.

2. Stir in the flour, adding more if necessary to make the dough easy to handle, although it will still be soft. Roll the dough into 1-inch balls. Chill thoroughly on a plate.

3. Mix all the filling ingredients together thoroughly, omitting powdered sugar.

4. Place a ball of chilled dough into a small tart pan and, with floured fingers, press over the base and up the sides of the pans. Repeat with all the balls of dough.

5. Spoon in the filling and bake for about 20-25 minutes at 350°F.

6. Allow to cool about 5 minutes and remove carefully from the pans. Cool completely on a wire rack before sprinkling with powdered sugar.

Step 4 Place a ball of dough in a small tart pan and, with floured fingers, press over the base and up the sides.

Step 5 Use a teaspoon to fill the tart pans, taking care not to get filling over the edge of the pastry.

Cook's Notes

Time
Preparation takes about 25 minutes. The dough will take at least 1 hour to chill thoroughly. Cooking takes about 20-25 minutes.

Cook's Tip
If the dough is too soft to handle afer mixing, chill for about 30 minutes or until easier to handle.

Serving Idea
Serve with coffee or tea or as petit fours after a formal dinner. The Tassies can be made in a larger size and served as a dessert with whipped cream.

SOUTHERN BISCUITS

Hot biscuits with butter and sometimes honey
are almost a symbol of Southern cooking, for breakfast,
lunch, dinner or all three!

1¾ cups all-purpose flour
½ tsp salt
2 tsps baking powder
1 tsp sugar
½ tsp baking soda
5 tbsps margarine or 4 tbsps shortening
¾ cup buttermilk

Step 5 Cut the dough into thick rounds with a plain pastry cutter.

Step 2 Rub the margarine into the flour until the mixture resembles coarse crumbs. Mix in enough milk to form a soft dough that can be handled.

1. Sift the flour, salt, baking powder, sugar and baking soda into a large bowl.

2. Rub in the margarine until the mixture resembles coarse crumbs.

3. Mix in enough buttermilk to form a soft dough. It may not be necessary to use all the milk.

4. Turn the dough out onto a floured surface and knead lightly until smooth.

5. Roll the dough out on a floured surface to a thickness of ½-¾ inch. Cut into rounds with a 2½-inch cookie cutter.

6. Place the circles of dough on a lightly-greased baking sheet about 1 inch apart. Bake in a preheated 450°F oven for 10-12 minutes. Serve hot.

Cook's Notes

Time
Preparation takes about 20 minutes and cooking takes about 10-12 minutes.

Cook's Tip
Biscuits freeze and·reheat well. Freeze for up to 3 months and thaw at room temperature. To reheat, wrap in foil and place in a moderate oven for about 5 minutes.

Serving Idea
Biscuits can be served hot for breakfast.

SPICED COOKIES

Crunchy and wholesome, these spicy cookies are a tea-time treat.

1 cup whole-wheat flour
½ tsp bicarbonate of soda
1 tsp ground cinnamon
1 tsp ground mixed spice
½ cup rolled oats
6 tbsps soft brown sugar
6 tbsps butter
1 tbsp corn syrup
1 tbsp milk

4. Divide the mixture into about 15 small balls. Place these onto lightly greased cookie sheets, keeping them well spaced, to allow the mixture to spread during baking.

5. Flatten each ball slightly with the back of a wetted spoon, and bake in a preheated oven, 350°F, for about 15 minutes, or until golden brown.

6. Allow the cookies to cool on the sheet before removing them.

Step 3 Pour the melted mixture into the dry ingredients and mix thoroughly to form a soft, pliable dough.

Step 5 Place the balls of cookie dough a little apart on the baking sheets, to allow for spreading. Flatten each ball slightly with the back of a wetted spoon.

1. Put the flour, bicarbonate of soda, cinnamon, mixed spice, oats and sugar into a bowl and stir well to blend thoroughly. Make a well in the middle.

2. In a small saucepan, melt the butter with the syrup and milk over a low heat.

3. Pour the melted mixture into the dry ingredients and beat well, until the mixture forms a smooth, pliable dough.

Step 6 Allow the cookies to cool before removing them from the baking sheet.

Cook's Notes

Time
Preparation takes about 20 minutes, and cooking takes about 15 minutes.

Cook's Tip
Heat a metal tablespoon, and use this to measure out the corn syrup, to avoid a sticky mess.

Serving Idea
Serve with ice cream or mousse.

DESERTS

It is worthwhile spending a little time decorating a dessert, since this completes the meal, and will thus often be the dish to linger in the memory long after the meal is over. However, it does not have to be a complicated decoration to impress. Indeed, the range of possibilities is vast, from a sprinkling of nuts, to frosted fruit and flowers or chocolate leaves.

EDIBLE FLOWERS

Fresh edible flowers tied together with fine ribbon are a pretty decoration for ices and chilled desserts. Make sure that the flowers are kept in water until you are just about to serve the dish, as they will wilt in hot weather.

Pat stems dry and place on the side of the plate just before serving. Try using marigolds and nasturtiums.

FROSTED FRUITS, FLOWERS, PETALS AND LEAVES

These make a really spectacular decoration that looks complicated, but is, in fact, very easy to

do. It is most important to use only edible leaves and flowers: if in doubt, leave

CARAMELIZED FRUIT

Fruit shining through a thin layer of light caramel makes a stunning decoration. Like frosted fruits, caramelized fruit should be used to decorate the dish at the last moment. To caramelize fruit, heat 1¼ cups water with 1lb sugar over a medium heat and stir until

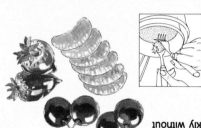

the sugar is dissolved. Boil quickly without

stirring until the syrup reaches the "hard crack" stage on a sugar thermometer, 300°-310°F. Remove from the heat. Using two oiled forks or skewers to hold the fruit, dip it into the sugar syrup to cover completely, and then place onto an oiled baking sheet. Do not touch the fruit with your fingers until it has cooled thoroughly, approximately 15 minutes.

CHOCOLATE

Chocolate can be used in many decorative ways. It can be finely or coarsely grated onto a dessert, or made into curls by scraping a block of chocolate with a potato peeler.

CHOCOLATE CARAQUE

Spread melted chocolate onto a marble slab or rimless baking sheet and, when it has set firmly, cut off thin "cigars" of chocolate using a sharp knife.

CHOCOLATE LEAVES

Wash rose or bay-leaves and dry well on paper towels. Brush the back of the leaves with melted chocolate and leave to set. Repeat this process

once more, and when the chocolate has completely set, carefully peel off each leaf, leaving its chocolate counterpart.

CREAM

Piped whipped cream adds a splendid finishing touch to a dessert. Take care not to overwhip the cream or it will become buttery. Keep the design

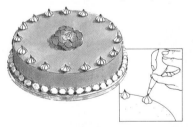

simple: a few rosettes beautifully piped are more effective than a mass of swirls. Top each rosette with a flaked nut, a frosted flower or petal, or a fresh raspberry or sliced strawberry.

them out! The following can be used, but ensure that they have not been sprayed with insecticides and that they are non-toxic: roses, violets, sweet peas, nasturtiums, primroses, and mint and borage leaves.

Wash the petals or flowers and pat them dry on paper towels. Dip them in, or brush with, lightly beaten egg white. Shake off the excess and then coat with a thick layer of superfine sugar. Leave to dry for about 1 hour on wax paper. This process is also perfect for fruits, including grapes, strawberries, plums and cherries. Frosted fruit should be added to the dish at the last minute, otherwise they will spoil.

FRUIT BASKETS

Melons and pineapples may be made into baskets to hold fruit salads, mousse and ice cream. For method, see citrus baskets in Garnishes for Appetizers. Oranges and lemons can be scooped out to hold sorbets or ice creams. Alternatively, melons and pineapples may be cut in half in a zig-zag fashion round the top of the fruit. The flesh is then carefully removed from both pieces, chopped and returned to its shell, with the top acting as a lid. An appropriate liqueur may be used to flavor the contents.

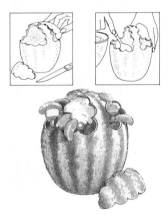